Praise For

Same God

At the end of the day, all we truly have is our story to tell or for others to tell on our behalf. Writing a memoir is not only admirable but a brave start to introducing oneself as an author. However, to be as honest and vulnerable as Tina is rare for African memoirists on the first try. The storytelling style adopted by Tina makes the reading easy and engaging. The story flows like a gentle stream that does not give too much away as it progresses.

As a spiritualist with a Christian background, I loved the manner in which she gives appropriate Biblical examples without watering down the message or twisting it to suit her view. She shares it as it is. As someone who had not read the Bible in a while, I was inspired to pick it up again and re-read the stories whilst juxtaposing them to my own life as she encouraged.

Same God is a book of encouragement, giving hope to women of all backgrounds, but particularly those that may be lost and discouraged by the decisions they made which turned out sour. In her conclusion, she states, *"Getting to fully understand what God wants you to do takes a lot of learning and unlearning."* Her story embodies this sentiment fully and I would say, let Tina speak to you from her heart and be encouraged.

—Hannah H. Tarindwa

Same God

Tina Butau

Published by KHARIS PUBLISHING, imprint of KHARIS MEDIA LLC.

Copyright © 2023 Tina Butau

ISBN-13: 978-1-63746-222-5

ISBN-10: 1-63746-222-0

Library of Congress Control Number: 2023942074

All KHARIS PUBLISHING products are available at special quantity discounts for bulk purchases for sales promotions, premiums, fund-raising, and educational needs. For details, contact:

Kharis Media LLC
Tel: 1-630-909-3405
support@kharispublishing.com
www.kharispublishing.com

Introduction

Habakkuk 2:2-3 NKJV

Then the LORD answered me and said: "Write the vision and make it plain on tablets, that he may run who reads it. For the vision is yet for an appointed time; But at the end, it will speak, and it will not lie. Though it tarries, wait for it; Because it will surely come, It will not tarry. (NKJV)

This is a memoir of my journey, describing where God took me from and how He brought me to where I am now. I sing along to the song Mercy by Maverick City a lot because "I am living proof of what the mercy of God can do."

I was led to write this book to share some of the hardships I endured in my life and how God was there for me and with me every step of the way. Even in times when I thought He had abandoned me, years later I looked back and saw that He was there in that moment. It describes in so much detail what I went through as a teen mum, as a single mother, as a woman and as a mother to a teenager. I dedicate this book to all women, single, married, widowed or divorced. As a single mother, there is a reason why you are single in this season; you need to find yourself as you try to figure out the lesson and the reason. As a married woman, you are still an individual who has their own personal journey with God, aside from the missional marriage you are in. Yes, I called marriage a mission because being married means you have someone whom God gave you to help you become the person God wants you to be, and vice versa. So, I wrote this book for all of us women. To share with you the seasons of my life and to use them to show how much God loves each one of us, even when it feels like He loves others more than you. You have heard people saying God has favourites, He makes life good and easy for the next person, but He leaves me to suffer. When we say that, we haven't encountered God. May my encounters with Him open your eyes to all your encounters that you may have missed because they didn't seem like God was even there in those moments.

God loves you and no, He hasn't abandoned you. Same God was written with godly women in mind; it feels like a comforting hug. It is a book that will show you the glory of God.

It shows the grace and patience the Lord afforded me in my quest to follow him. My name is Tina, and it means Follower of Christ, so as I follow Him, I was tasked with journaling some of the things I endured in my journey. I have written this book as the seasons of my life, and I share in it how I overcame or didn't. It has numerous testimonies that aim to help you the reader in strengthening your faith in God. I have noticed that for every season of my life, someone in the bible has already gone through it and so for me to figure out how to respond to that season I am in, I study that biblical character that resonates with me in that particular season. The Bible was meant to be our guide too, for us to do or not do what some of the people of God did, to learn from it. Some seasons will only show me who I was long after that season has passed, but I can still draw lessons from it, nonetheless.

This book serves to remind you that God is unchanging. He is the Same God that parted the Red Sea and the same God that made a shepherd boy courageous. He is the same God of Abraham, Isaac, and Jacob. He still performs miracles today in our lives as He did in the biblical days. Most people think miracles were only happening back in those days but after reading this book, you will be able to look deep into your life and see some of the miracles God has done for you, but you may not have acknowledged them as miracles because we expect a fire to come out of a rock as it did for Gideon. We expect the sea to be parted, not recognizing that God may already be parting seas for us. We want to see young David defeating Goliath, and we don't see how God is removing some giants in our lives who may not be Goliath but are giants all the same. He is still making promises like He did with Abraham and Sarah and fulfilling them too. He still talks to us, as He did with Moses, He may not appear as a burning bush, but He left us the Holy Spirit and as such, we are able to converse with him as Moses did. Read Same God and go with me on an emotional yet rewarding journey. Brace yourself and I will see you in the chapters to come. This Same God is as much in my life as He is in yours. Come, let's learn about Him together.

Acknowledgements

I want to thank the Lord for giving me the strength and courage to write some of the most sensitive and personal things of my life to support someone who may be going through the same. It was not easy to bare my soul for the whole world to see, but God made me understand that the things written here bring Him and only Him all the glory. He chose me in all my unworthiness to show his people how He is the Same God whose love endures through generations.

I want to thank my friend Kudzai for cheering me on; years ago, she kept urging me to write a book. I guess the time then wasn't right but thank you for planting that seed in me. To my friends Emily & Sis Bertha who picked up my calls anytime I needed to talk about my book, thank you. You two know the frustrations I had, the confusion of what to write and what not to write. The late-night calls to give me support. I appreciate you. Thank you, Emily, for being my consistent friend and for wiping the tears off my cheeks when I opened my old wounds to write them down. Thank you for holding my hand while revisiting the darkest places of my past. Your encouraging words and advice kept me going. To my daughter Chikomborero, what would I have ever done without you? Thank you for turning off the TV and barking at me to "Go and write." Thank you for being an overall blessing in my life. Thank you for cheering me on. My friend Jo, you are important to me. Your support was phenomenal. Listening to me and reading the book when it was still a skeleton and telling me how much potential it had gave me the strength to carry on. Thank you.

Prologue

Proverbs 3:5-6
"Trust in the Lord with all your heart, and do not lean on your own understanding. In all your ways acknowledge him, and he will make straights your paths."

Happily, unaware that I would be a mother in 7 months, I smiled at my sister Eve while daydreaming of becoming a pharmacist. She must have been saying something to me, but all I could hear were mumbles. She caught my attention with a sharp laugh, one that pierced my ears. It was at that moment that I realized I was meant to laugh too, and so I did. It was stupid to laugh, unaware of what she had said, but I chose to be stupid than to have been caught that I wasn't listening to whatever she was talking about.

I decided to end my daydream and we both walked outside. In between our houses was a fence that didn't serve its purpose, so our neighbour Mai Masanhi beamed at us as she said good morning. As I was about to say good morning back, she ghasted, jumped a step back with her eyes popping open and said, "AH, Tina, is that pregnancy I see?" In dismay, I looked down at my tiny belly. You see, I was a very scrawny teen with very little body mass to hold a fetus. I was confused and said, "No, I cannot be pregnant; what made you think that way?" I had "barely" had intercourse with my boyfriend Frank, so this didn't make sense. Didn't they say you had to have really indulged in this adult act for one to become pregnant?

As I was still trying to make sense of all this, she told me to take out my left breast and pinch the nipple. "If whitish discharge comes out then that will be your answer, "she said in a low steady voice. I did this as my hands shook, and Eve just stood right there, mortified. I pinched my nipple and surely, some fluid emerged. At this moment I felt shivers down my spine; it felt as though I was drowning. "This can't be right." I crooned. Reality hit hard. That night, a couple of weeks ago I had indeed become pregnant. I was just a child, about to have a child. I couldn't comprehend what had happened. How was I going to tell my mother?

A lot of feelings washed over me as I sat on the ground to try and fathom my new reality. I was just in my first year in college, the first semester to be precise. I wanted to quite simply, scream. Eve began telling me my options, but a new feeling had taken over. It was love. I should have been scared but my heart instantly became full. I was going to be a mother. I imagined myself bathing my baby in a pink baby dish with Johnson's baby products on the side. I wished for a girl. Eve was again, mumbling while I daydreamed of breastfeeding a tiny human being. With newfound love radiating through me, I looked at my sister to finally listen to what she had to say. We had to find a way to share the news with my boyfriend. I got up and Eve hugged me and held me in that position as I breathed deeply and wept quietly.

Distraught, I went inside trying to find a way to break it down to my mother and grandmother. My grandmother was a bubbly woman who had no sensor in her mouth. She said things as they were, regardless of how one would take it. She had a crazy sense of humour and was full of jokes. She was also the most loving woman I knew. She had a very light complexion for an aged black woman with hazel brown eyes that seemed to be smiling constantly but today, it was as though the light and smile had vanished from her eyes. Her scattered freckles seemed to be more defined today because the colour in her face was gone. When I walked into the room, the atmosphere became tense as I walked slowly with my head down toward her.

I ambled with the little energy that I had, shaking; my eyes met that of Gogo. I thought her eyes looked bluer than brown, but that was before I realized that it was a reflection of a tear. She let out a deep and heavy sigh; she must have wiped the tear before it escaped her eyelids. She didn't speak, she simply gave me a dead stare & I imagine that at that moment, she was thinking of how she would tell the women she mentored in the church that her eldest granddaughter had become pregnant out of wedlock. Her face showed a tightness that seemed to have been connected to her gut because really, her gut had sunk, and it showed on the core of her face. I knew less of what would happen to me at that moment than a flea knew about the breed of the dog it bit. She stood and said quite simply, "Follow me into the bedroom."

I obliged and knelt in front of her as she sat on her bed. She said, "Remove your top and come closer." I couldn't waste her time gawking and pondering, so I quickly removed the pink t-shirt that I had on. She adeptly examined my belly and breasts, then sighed once more. This old woman was wise. She didn't need to do a pregnancy test to be convinced that I was pregnant. She put her forefinger deep inside my belly button. You'd imagine it was painful, but no, all I felt was pressure. She cleared her throat and called out for Eve as loudly as she could in her groggy voice. It wasn't usually groggy, but I suppose this was caused by the lump-in-the-thought feeling that she had. Eve walked in and shut the door behind her; she knelt beside me and said, "Yes Gogo, you called me?" "Run fast to Mbuya Mugwadi's house, tell her to come now because there is an emergency. From there, go all the way to my son Charles' house and ask him and his wife to come here right away." Here and now, I knew that things had gotten real. In the Zimbabwean culture, your mother's brother and his wife are the only people that are "qualified" to address bedroom issues and in this case, one had arisen. Mbuya Mugwadi was Gogo's friend, who was dark in complexion and had breasts big enough to need two bras to hold. That was her most pronounced body feature. She thought she was funny, but she annoyed me with her silly jokes. She lived only 5 houses away, so she was in the bedroom with us within minutes.

"Janet's child is pregnant my friend; I have already examined her. We are waiting for her uncle and his wife to come, then you and them can take her to her boyfriend's place as per culture." Gogo said. That lady with her jokes looked towards me with a smug smile on her wrinkled face and said, "You can tell me who your boyfriend is. Is he handsome, was he great in bed? All this was said while she was nudging me with her elbow. I wanted to quite simply slap her. I replied as calmly as I could and said, "his name is Frank; he works at the shops that we pass through on our way from church." I was terrified as I spoke these words, but I had to, nonetheless. As we waited for my uncle and his wife to arrive, Gogo called my mother into the bedroom. I thought to myself, oh oh! I had forgotten about the one person that mattered. What will I tell my mother? Regret began to wash over me. The door opened and she said, "Tina..." The sad croaking sound of her voice appalled me. I will never forget the sight that greeted me when she walked in. Her mouth bowed up when she glanced at me, and I quickly arose to join her in a tearful hug. As I was in her bosom, I wept. Her pretty mouth went gray, flat, and hard. Though tears trickled down her cheeks, she managed to say, "It's okay," as she stroked my braids.

She then said, "Tina, what happened to the dreams you had, that wedding you wanted on a beach with the bluest waters? What happened to the cake that my aunt was going to bake for your wedding? You have disappointed me in ways I cannot begin to explain." In my heart, I kept murmuring the words, "I know, I Know."

Table Of Contents

Chapter - 1

The Joseph Season of My Life

"In the fullness of time, I, the Lord will make it happen."

Isaiah 60:22

A girl with a dream. Tina at 3 years

The Butau's, Janet and Albert made their living from electronics shop they owned. My father Albert wanted me and my only sibling, Shaima, to be in the shop. My brother is an only son and he quite enjoyed electronic engineering while I fancied myself a receptionist of sorts. My father was proud of his company and clung to it as he'd clung to his desire to be rich. My father longed for a lavish life, so he relocated to this small town rich in gold about 12 years ago. Mining towns made for wealthy people; wealthy people were good for his business. He was a tad bit taller than an average man but spread the height on a brawny frame. He was a handsome fellow in the conventional sense. He had a way with words and people and used his charm to get whatever he wanted. This ambitious man wanted the best for his children, so he took us both to A schools. He had many projects running apart from his shop. He also loved poultry. My parents gave us a good life and supported my dreams from a very young age. I had the desire to venture into culinary arts since I was 9. It is true that the Lord puts desires in our hearts to guide us into the life He plans for us.

My father was an idealist who had ways to bring anything he thought to life. I am talking about a man who built, from scratch, an indoor glass aquarium for our living room. He saw it somewhere, and he knew he had to have it. He was quite the handyman. In his selflessness, my dad ignited the fantasist who lay dormant inside of me. He would ask me almost every night to go for a walk with him and sit on a concrete bench-like slab near a footbridge. "Let's go pa bridge, Tina," he would say. I used to love it because at that bridge, my father would enthrall me by letting me fantasize and he would go inside of that fantasy with me. Dad would say, "Close your eyes, imagine the store you'd want and take me there." A smiling me would smile with eyes tightly shut and say, "So, this is a double-storey coffee shop. As you open the entrance door on the ground floor, you are welcomed by the scent of freshly baked cakes. To the right, there is a wide food display carrying a variety of cake slices and sweet desserts. To the left, there will be a few sets of tiny tables and chairs for those who want to have coffee in the shop." "Uh huh," Dad would urge. From the motivation, I would continue and say, "Then you go upstairs and there you will see a cake display. I will have cakes for different occasions. You need to find someone who can create dummy cakes. I want one that will be made into a cat with a tear on its cheek." He would straighten his posture and move his face closer in a gesture to show that he is paying attention and to slightly compel me to keep reaching further into my fantasy.

"Okay, hear me out; I am doing cakes for all occasions, not just birthdays and weddings. The cat cake is called the I'm Sorry cake; one can get this one when trying to apologize. It is a sweet gesture. So, I am having different cakes for different purposes." I went on to talk about the different dummy cakes that would be on display and how the corner had flowers and cards to go with the different types of cakes. When I snapped out of my daydream, he said, "You won't be able to bake using the conventional oven, so I am going to build you one." Ecstatic, I screamed and jumped because I knew that not only was this man whom I called Dad capable of creating an industrial-grade oven for me, but I also knew that he didn't think my dream was unrealistic. He knew what my passion was and nurtured it. A lot of promises were made "pa bridge." My father was my hero. You see, his name was Albert and he named me Albertina. I was the apple of his eye, and he would talk about me every time.

You could equate me with Joseph, as I had a dream and my father had set on a journey to create for me a "coat of many colours" In this instance, it was the oven he had begun building for me. It was nothing as I had seen before. You see, this man was very intentional about loving me. He was like no other dad I had seen before, not your typical African dad. He would profess his love for me to anyone and everyone who cared to listen, and he spoke very highly of me with so much adoration. My confidence was boosted by him in ways I cannot begin to explain.

When I turned 14, I had a cooking final exam for my food and nutrition class. We were given meals to cook and when I went home, I told my parents, who then bought me the ingredients to practice cooking the meals while being timed. We did this for 3 days. I did very well on the final exam, and I got an A for food & nutrition. God allowed my parents to see what I was passionate about and they encouraged me. Now I am a seasoned chef and baker, thanks to my parents. When I was in grade 5 and only 9 years old, my mother made me bake a cake she took to a school ruffle show to sell. It sold fast and people asked for recipes. My mom would proudly announce that "It was Tina who baked this, not me." That gave me confidence and I knew I could do anything because my parents had told me since I was young that the sky was the limit.

Oblivious of how my life would never be the same within a few minutes, I walked into my dad's office with a beaming smile and sat on his lap as I had done for the past 15 years of my life. He would kiss my cheek and ask how my day went. People thought it inappropriate for a teenager to still be sitting on her father's lap, but my dad was willful when it came to how he showed me love; it was as if he knew that he would leave and so he wanted to give me all the love he could before he left. He said, "Let's go somewhere; there is something I need to show you." I thought it could have been something to do with Indulgence, my coffee shop, as he had begun preparing for it, or so he would say. We got to where we were going, and it was the hospital. I was confused but walked in all the same. We got into a room, and Mai Morris, a woman I had been introduced to once as his newest business partner, was sitting on the hospital bed. I didn't know what was going on, but my stomach began to churn. Mai Morris looked at me and then at my dad as if she was signaling him to say something. With a weak smile, Dad then said, "Tina, this is your new baby sister, doesn't she look just like you?" "I, I, I I'm sorry, come again"? I stammered with pure disbelief in my voice. What had this man just said to me? I felt hot, and then instantly very cold; I got dizzy and felt a sinking feeling in my gut, as if I just came off a roller coaster type of feeling. Tears stung the back of my eyes as I looked at the tiny fragile baby that my dad, my father now held in his arms. I listened to him and the mother of his child giggling softly. There was happiness in his eyes. But wait, I thought to myself, wasn't I his happy place? Could someone else make his eyes smile like that? I thought that smile belonged to me and only me. Was I dreaming? His baby's mother looked at me and said, "We decided to name her Mary after your dad's sister." She said this all the while beaming with joy. She went on to tell me that my father was playing a UB40 song for her. At that moment, the tears came now fell down my cheeks like rain as I lurched across the room to sit in the chair that was in the corner. Why was I crying? Was I happy that I was now a big sister or was I grieving for a father that I had just clearly lost? I do not know. I do know that at the moment, I quite simply wanted to die. He what? Played our song to his new daughter? But I thought that track was mine. He kept kissing her tiny cheeks; I couldn't understand. Didn't that kiss belong to me? I saw my world crumbling right before my eyes.

"Why are you crying Tina?" He reached down and touched my face with one hand. I was boiling inside. He dared to ask me WHY I was crying. Really? I made a straight face, choked on my voice that was groggier than that of a frog and said, "I'm just happy; they're tears of joy." I lied right through my teeth as I watched my sister's mum adjust herself in her bed while her child slept in her arms, like an angel, very peaceful. I gathered the little energy that I still had in me and left the hospital to run to my mommy. I just wanted my mum.

As soon as I got to her, I blurted out and said, "Dad has a child now with your friend. He went with me to the hospital, and they showed off their child to me." My mum's face instantly turned gray, literally. She fell to her knees and wept. She walked to the window and looked out as if to not let her eyes meet mine. "When I heard it," she muttered, "I almost didn't believe it." She glanced back at me and hoped I was strong enough for what she wanted to say next. "I can't imagine what you must be going through," she began, "I know what your father means to you. I didn't know how to tell you, but all those days he would be gone; that is where he was. I protected you and your brother from that." On this day, in August of that year, my life changed; my dreams were crushed, my heart was shattered, and all hope was gone. A light turned off inside me, never to be lit again.

My father left us and went to live with his new family in a different country altogether. I was heartbroken. The first heartbreak I ever got from a man was from my father. He just went, just like that and never said goodbye. I was angry, and I was hurt but my mother was in a worse state. She had this kindness about her, and it was the bulk of her temperament. You see, from all this, Mum had a stroke and lost her speech. She couldn't talk for days. She lost her mobility and stopped working. She was a quiet lady, and I hear quiet people tend to bottle up their feelings and they consume them from the inside. Mum was a full-figured woman with a coca cola bottle shape, short but with pronounced features. She didn't keep long hair like other women; she always had her short 4c hair dyed midnight black and trimmed into a neat boy cut that did well to accentuate her oval-shaped face. Her eyebrows were arched as if she had been born with a natural cut crease. She wore prescription sunglasses and had a single black wart above her left cheek; it was her beauty mark. This beautiful woman was devastated. Her husband had left her to be with another woman. She took numerous sessions of therapy and when she got out of the hospital, she was taken to her mother's house, as she no longer had her matrimonial home. She moved into her mother's house with me but unfortunately, there wasn't enough space for my brother to come too, so she asked the church pastor, Mufundisi Chabvura to house her son until she had made a plan. But what plan could Mum make? She couldn't even walk without mobility aids.

Life as I knew it changed drastically. At my grandma's house, we lived with three of my cousins; one was older than me, my sister Eve. In the African culture, we rarely say cousin. It is a sister. So, there was Eve, me, Charlene, and Tanya. It was now impossible for me to remain as spoilt as I was at my parent's house. I had to toughen up to survive my new reality. Gogo raised us with so much love. She made sure we were all fed and no one lacked. She was too old to work, so she didn't have a job but fed us what her children in the diaspora would buy for her. Her husband was there, a no-nonsense guy. Growing up, gogo taught all of us ways of how to become better people and raised us as Christians. We would go to church choir; youth camps and she nurtured me into being the Proverbs 31 woman that we will read about in a few chapters to come.

One day as we were walking from Church with Eve, we passed the low-density shopping complex that anchored our Rimuka township; we stopped by to see Eve's friend who worked in the hair salon. As we were chatting and laughing, a guy who smelled of bergamot and sandalwood walked in. His cleanliness and aura demanded our attention. He was a dark-skinned chap with full abs and a chest that showed how much time he spent at the gym lifting weights. He looked like those dark guys that smear oil all over their bodies and model in magazines. He wore a white, dramatically white t-shirt written Billabong in black. His eyes were framed by thick, dark lashes, embowed over by expressive brows. He had red eyes for some reason, with a halo of dark brown ringing the pupil. He looked at me and instantly looked down as a shy person would. "Ahem," he cleared his throat and bluntly said to me. "Hi, what is your name?" This man didn't even have a pickup line. I rolled my eyes and he saw it and then went on to say, "A beautiful girl like you shouldn't ignore people. Can you give me your landline number and I will ring you later." He added. I wasn't sure; I thought guys with a body like his were pompous. They did too much you know. I was bent on ignoring him, then this guy went on to pull out a crisp $50 bill and handed it to me. Now, that got my attention. I looked over and said, "What is this for?" all the while trying to not show my excitement. "It's for you to take a taxi home. Beautiful girls cannot work. Either taxi or I can drop you off; that is my car." He said while pointing at a black VW Golf that was parked meters away. I took the money and smiled while trying to write down our phone number with a pen that didn't work. "22799; try to cram the number coz your silly pen isn't working." He smiled, for he knew he had won. Eve was pretending to not see this, but I could tell she was dying for us to start roasting the guy. We went home and we were so excited. This guy gave us all that for a $3 taxi. He sounded like our Prince Charming because we needed the money. His name was Frank, and he had just gotten himself a new girlfriend. He didn't ask me out; we just kind of began dating.

With our new richness, Eve and I went to buy a crate of eggs, potatoes, panties, and a new bathing towel. We had one towel that was once blue and white, in the size of an A4 paper. It had now turned almost khaki because of the hard water that we used to bathe. We walked every day about a kilometre away from the house to fetch water from the community borehole. We'd carry the 20-litre buckets on our heads, and a 5-litre would hang on the free hand. We would do 3 or 4 of these trips to get water for everyone and we would keep a single bucket for ourselves to bathe. Somehow, that water was enough for me and my sister to wash using our tattered towel.

So, dating Frank proved to be beneficial. He was so generous. Gogo couldn't afford to get us most of the things we needed, so he chipped in and began helping me financially. Sometimes he would bring his car to take us to the borehole so that we wouldn't need to carry the buckets on our heads. Gogo didn't know I had a boyfriend; we had to be discreet. A few months passed and he asked me to go to his house. I cringed because I knew what it meant. He was far much older than I was, he was 26 and I was 18. I spent days refusing then Eve convinced me that it would be okay. I was disturbingly very bony and dainty. I would wear a 14-year-old's clothes at 18. I had scanty hair, so it could only hold very few braids. I would always have bangs with my braids to conceal my big forehead. Despite my not-so-appealing bodily figure, Frank seemed to be attracted to me. So, on this day, I agreed to sneak out of the house and go to spend the night with him. I asked him to promise he wouldn't try to touch me through the night, and I got some sort of false comfort from hearing him say he will be a gentleman. We got to his house; it was so clean I didn't even know where to step. His floors shone as though someone had poured a glossy substance on them. His bed was made like the ones in hotels, and everything was so organized. He was the first OCD person I had met, I used to read about it but right now I was in one of those houses. He made me a cup of tea while he made a quick snack. He then told me that we could both sleep on the bed with different blankets.

I was crazy to believe I had the situation under control because before I knew it, this guy began kissing me as I fought him off and one thing led to another, and my virginity was broken. I don't know how it happened because I was fighting him the entire time and all I could feel was pain. The wrestling and the adult deed were all over before I could fathom everything that had happened.

I furiously asked him to drive me back that night and when I got home, I told Eve what had happened, and she assured me that I was not pregnant. The following day, Frank came and gave me money and told me to go and buy the morning-after pills. Eve said I didn't need them since she was certain that from how I explained what had happened, there was no way I could have been pregnant, so we spent the money on Marie biscuits! Eve couldn't have been more wrong because 2 months later, our neighbour saw that I was pregnant. I hadn't seen Frank again since that time, so I instantly knew that it was indeed that night that got me here. Fear, sadness, and despair ran over me.

Joseph the Dreamer

"But there is a God in heaven who reveals mysteries.
He has shown King Nebuchadnezzar what will happen in days to come.
Your dream and the visions that passed through your mind
as you were lying in bed are these."

Daniel 2:28

God showed Joseph what his future held in a dream. At the time, Joseph had no idea what that dream meant, but the Lord put it in his heart anyway. Sometimes, God puts a dream in our hearts to lead us to where He wills us to be. A vision/dream/prophecy from God is the Lord letting you in on his plan for your life, not that he needs you to do anything about it, take this as a father promising that he will build a car for his son; he has the capacity and potential to do so. When he begins building the car, he asks his son to join him in the assembly of parts. He is doing this so that he can yield a relationship with his son while he lets him in on how he is building the car. Can he do it without the son's knowledge and help? Absolutely. He is using this time to bond with hisson. That is why God puts a vision in our lives. One day, you look back, and you will see how the Lord was with you every step of the way and how it was done in a way that shows his glory. For Joseph to be where he was, he had to pass through all the places he did. He had to endure every pain. If Joseph hadn't been removed from the life he knew with his parents, he wouldn't have been the man he had become. Sometimes the things that we think are in our lives to destroy us are propelling us to move forward until we reach our promised land. I call this my Joseph chapter because I too was a dreamer. At that time, I didn't know anything about culinary arts, but I spoke of it in a way that felt like I knew what I was talking about. I didn't know that 23 years later, just like Joseph's dream happened 23 years later, I would become a business owner with a gourmet cooking company. I didn't know I would be an interior designer. I may have designed that shop in my head many years ago due to the desire the Lord put in my heart, but I didn't know that I was actually sharing my dreams with my father. Like Joseph, I was innocently saying what I saw. For Joseph, he saw it in a dream. For me, I saw this in the depths of my imagination. Let's pause a little while and go further into this. I was only 10 years old, could my imagination have been so vivid that I spoke of things that I hadn't ever seen in so much detail or was the Lord gracious to me so much so that He gave me a clear and precise vision about something that would actually happen in my life

23 years later? I am currently living in that vision. I have realized from this season that if God says it, then He will do it. It may take years, it may take rocky roads but eventually, God prevails. His word will not return void and He will see to it that He performs it as He said He would. Isaiah 55:11. God allows the things that happen in our lives to test us and develop our faith. We sometimes have to pass through every one of the things that we do because they help us become the people God intends us to be.

Chapter - 2

The Jeremiah Season of My Life.

"Every good and perfect gift is from above, coming down from the Father of the heavenly lights, who does not change like shifting shadows."

James 1:17

(Continuation from prologue) Gogo and her friend both examined me in the bedroom and when they were certain that I was indeed pregnant, they began packing my bag to take me to my boyfriend's house. My uncle and his wife came, and we made our way to "Machimbini," it was the area where Frank's grandmother and he sometimes lived so I was supposed to be taken to a place where the elders resided. "Pack your bags muzukuru; you made your bed the day you removed your clothes for a man, now lie in it," my uncle said in a very stern voice. I didn't know that a person could cry inside; that is all I was doing the entire time. I obliged and said goodbye to my weeping mother who had refused to eat that night. I packed my clothes into a plastic bag; I had nowhere else to put them. Even if I wanted a bag, how many clothes did I even have? I can tell you that all the clothes in my life were no more than 10. With all my belongings tightly clutched just below my chest, we walked in loud silence for 30 minutes. "Cover her head with that blanket before we get into the gate, and make sure you knock loudly." Mbuya Mugwadi said to my uncle's wife. "Tisvikewo panoooo," she shouted saying "we have arrived," at the top of her voice. A dumbfounded me was just covered in that heavy blanket, sweating & wondering what was going on. She must have picked up a rock to use to knock on the gate because I then heard the loud tapping of rock hitting metal. A few moments later, an old lady came out and asked us to come in. It was pretty obvious why we were there; that blanket over my head told them everything they needed to know. I had come to elope. My uncle's wife helped me to sit on the ground and whispered in my ear that we needed to sit outside, and that was tradition. I learnt a lot more about Shona culture in those 5 minutes than I had in my entire life. "We see that you have come with a covered bride, so I am assuming one of my boys made her pregnant; which of the three is it?" a woman I could not see muttered. At that moment I heard clapping, not the applause type of clap; it was the Shona hollow clap that is done by closing your hands together, making an arch with your fingers, and then clapping. It is a traditional clap that signifies respect. "Thank you for letting us in; the man responsible for making our daughter pregnant is your grandson, Frank." I heard my uncle say a little louder so that his voice could override the sound of the clap they were still doing. I began to sweat even more, not sure if it was from the blanket that was still over my head or if it was the heat from a boiling me; nonetheless, I was drenched in sweat. "Fraaaaaaaaank, come here," his grandma screamed into the phone at the top of her lungs in an agitated voice. We just sat there in silence while we waited for him to come. 10 minutes later, I heard footsteps and a voice I recognized saying, "What is Gogo, I swear I didn't make anyone pregnant." "Shut up and uncover the poor girl, stupid boy, hurry up." You see, they had to remove the blanket as one uncovers the wedding veil. Disgust is what ran through me when he was slowly removing the blanket. I was angry at myself. So, the first time I am going to experience a "veil" opening is when I'm sitting in the dust in the most ghetto part of our neighbourhood in the presence of an old woman I loathed, my uncle and his wife and this old woman that was talking? I wished for that ground to swallow me whole. I wished to disappear. I was brought back to reality with light flooding my face as Frank took off the last part of the blanket. "Urgh! Tina? What is this?" Frank said in disbelief, with actual shock on his face. "Did you expect someone else? How many other women did you sleep with other than my niece?" my uncle asked with horror in his voice. I wanted to cry; I just wanted my mother; I wanted to go back home. "Talk," his grandmother said while giving him serious slaps on his shoulder.

"If this girl is pregnant, it isn't mine. I said I'm not responsible." Frank said in protest while throwing his hands in the air. The atmosphere became tense. "It can't be," he repeated; I gave her money to buy morning-after pills and she said she took them. I asked her and she said she did and then I never saw her again. I slept with her once, and she took the pill, so how then am I responsible for this?" he crooned. With eyes about to drop into the ground, I was faced with the conundrum of trying to figure out how I was going to explain that we bought biscuits with the money intended for the pills because Eve said I couldn't have been pregnant.

Embarrassment washed over & then I made a straight face and said in a very low voice, "I didn't take the pills. Eve said what we did couldn't have made me pregnant, so we bought biscuits with the money." They all laughed, all of them except for Frank. There were tears in his eyes. I reached out to touch him and he threw my hand away before he said, "Gogo, this isn't mine, they are wasting my time and I am going back." As he took a step to leave, Mbuya Mugwadi dramatically pulled him back by clenching his trousers at the waistline. "Come paniolo, where the hell do you think you are going? When you were ejaculating, did you think you were doing it in an empty tin of baked beans? Stupid boy, you are going to marry our daughter whether you want or not." She said in an angry way that made all of us think, "Oh, oh." Now the atmosphere was purely hostile. My relatives said they would leave me there, and if they wanted me to sleep outside, it was their call. They left. When they went, Frank told his grandma that he didn't believe me and so he left too and went to his house. His grandmother was extremely kind to me; may God rest her beautiful soul. She told me to come in and she housed me for days, explaining that Frank would come back for me once he got back to his senses. Days became weeks and weeks became a month and he never came for me. I couldn't keep staying there, it wasn't his house, so I made contact with my brother and asked him to talk to my grandparents to ask them to take me back. They refused. They didn't refuse because they were mean but because culture dictated their actions. As per Zimbabwean culture, I had to be at my baby's father's house. It was beyond my grandparent's control. This is what happens to everyone if they get pregnant out of wedlock.

I left Frank's grandma's place because I was no longer welcome since he hadn't returned to get me. I began going door to door to my mother's friends. Some kicked me out, some gave me food but refused to shelter me, and some would just tell me frankly to leave. I became destitute, with nowhere to go. So, I would spend my days at one growth point named Rumwe; I had made a friend there, a man who was repairing shoes. His name was Malcolm; everyone in the ghetto called him 'Macum.' So, I would sit on the bench with Macum and he would share with me his chibuku.

Chibuku is a thick food and drink low percentage acholic beverage made out of maize and sorghum. See the picture in insert. It would sustain me through the day then in the evenings, I would go back home to my grandma to sleep. You might imagine I was now welcome there. No, Eve and Tanya would help me sneak into the house through the back door when everyone had slept. I would jump the fence from our neighbour's house; then Eve would pretend as though she was going to throw away garbage in the back then she would  let me in. I would sleep with my mum; I had a small bucket that they made into a chamber pot for me so that I wouldn't go to the bathroom and risk being caught going to the washroom. This went on for a month and then Eve came up with a grand plan. The plan this time was go to Frank's house and tie me in there so he couldn't make me leave. So, we went to Macum, my friend and asked him to find a long chain for me, as long as he could and two locks with keys. Macum came through. I went to Frank's house at a time when I knew he would be cleaning his car; remember his OCD? Yes, he cleaned his car every single morning. I went there and went in because there was no way his door would have been locked when he was there. I took the chain and chained myself to the window burglar bar. The chain was tied and locked to my wrist on one end, then tied and locked at the other end. It was very long so I had enough length to enable me to sleep on the bed and reach for a few things. I tried to swallow the key, but it was too big, don't laugh; desperate times call for desperate measures. So instead, I put the key in my hair. Frank came in singing his reggae song and got the shock of his life seeing me chained to his window. He laughed so hard that even I began laughing with him.

He politely asked for the key, and I told him I swallowed it. "I knew you were smart, but this takes the cup. Even if you had glued yourself to my floor, I would have found a way to remove you and take you out of my house. I told you I didn't want you because the baby you are carrying isn't mine." He said with a frown on his face. He called his friends, and they came to see him, and all laughed at me. It was so embarrassing; I wanted to die. Why wouldn't God just take me? Sadly, death doesn't come when you most need it. His other friend came moments after with a bolt cutter and cut the bar I was chained on. He chased me out and locked his door and left me standing right there. I spent the day there, with no food and when he came back in the evening, he found me there and left me there. He acted as if I was invisible. I slept outside. I had to cover myself with the foot rug that was at his door. In the morning he left me there. This man jumped over my body that was cuddled up into a ball. I cried so much that morning but again, pain doesn't kill you when your wish is to just cease to exist. I prayed as I cried, asking God where he was and questioning why he hated me so much. At this point, I was desperate for God to show up, but He did not. I spent the afternoon on the same door, hoping that maybe if Frank returned, he would feel sorry for me and let me in. As I was waiting for him to come back, his neighbour came and said, "We saw you sleeping here last night, don't you have a family? This guy will not take you in; go home." I tearfully explained that I couldn't return home but gave her my brother's phone number. The loneliness and wandering depressed me; there was nothing I could do except just cry. Tears had gotten to a stage where they wouldn't flow; I would simply groan. The neighbour reached out to my brother and told him the situation I was in. I am told that my only sibling went to my grandparents, knelt on the ground, and pleaded for my life. Eve said she had never seen anyone who cried so much, not even at a funeral. He asked them to shelter me until I had given birth and after that, I would find a job and find a place for me and my child. My grandfather explained that he had heard that I was suffering and that he wasn't paying a deaf ear out of spite, but it was culture and also because my father wasn't there and if anything had happened, my father's family would have blamed them. He said that out of love he would forgo what culture states and take me back in, on a condition that my relatives from my father's side were told. My brother is said to have assured him that he would take responsibility if anything happened and that he was taking on the role of the father in my life. Such love. And so, I went back home after 4 months in the wilderness.

My grandmother took great care of me. She would make me tea meant for pregnant women, porridge, and all the stuff that pregnant women get. Tanya and Eve would take turns bathing me because my belly was very big, and I couldn't reach for my toes. Mum would do what she could in her state, but I was surrounded with love. One day, I was sitting with Eve on the veranda, and I had a vision. At that moment, I didn't know that I had the capability of tapping into my future. I remember this vividly; I said to her, "Eve, a lot of people told me to abort this pregnancy. When I was going around to people's houses, some would bluntly say, "Terminate this baby so you can go back home." I refused because this child is my gift from God; she is going to be a blessing, not just to me but to everyone around me and for that reason, I am naming her Chikomborero, meaning Blessing in Shona." Realize that I said she; I just knew it was a she. When I was about to give birth, a lady that was once our maid came to visit my mum; when she was told that the man responsible didn't want anything to do with it, she said to me and my mum, "I know of a pastor who performs miracles from the church that I go to. I can go with Tina immediately and I can definitely tell you that the man responsible will most certainly marry her in a few days." This news gave me hope and I went along with her. This pastor was known to return the teeth that had fallen out of older people's mouths and tell you everything about your past, what you ate today, or what your ID number was.

Everyone in Kadoma had heard about pastor Sandam. He said that I was going to be married to the father of my child within a month. I was so excited, and I put my hope and trust in this pastor. Months came and went; I was still unmarried. I was devastated and I remember telling my mum that this guy had promised to do everything in his power. I got over it and accepted the reality that I was going to be a single mother.

"What if troubles of this life are your mercies in disguise?"
Stand Music

"For I know the plans I have for you," declares the LORD, "plans to prosper you and not to harm you, plans to give you hope and a future. Then you will call on me and come and pray to me, and I will listen to you. You will seek me and find me when you seek me with all your heart."

Jeremiah 29:11-13

This was the Jeremiah season of my life. Just like Jeremiah, all I was concerned about was wanting to be married and didn't want to find out why God was saying no. I wanted what I wanted without stopping to see that the rejection may have been a blessing. We have our perception of blessings so when they come in a different form than what we expect, we miss them and conclude that it is a curse; but what if the very thing that is making us lose sleep at night is the actual blessing and not what we want? What if God is saving us from denying us the very thing that we think we need? (Listen to the song by Stand Music – Blessings)

Jeremiah had made plans and announced to his father that he intended to marry his girlfriend that he loved, Judith. He was thrilled at the prospect of marriage, and he was ready to help remove his bride's father from debt. He had his plans, and he was working towards them. Jeremiah wanted to turn to prophets because he hoped they would tell him something that supported his desire to be married; he just needed someone who was not God to give him something he could cling onto. Just like when I went to that pastor, I wanted him to tell me what I wanted to hear. I wanted to put the situation in my hands. Being told about all the 'miraculous' things this pastor could do gave me hope. (I'm rolling my eyes) Jeremiah knew the answer already but a part of him wanted to be told something that he wanted to hear. People who preach telling us that if we are having problems or if we are depressed as Christians, it means that we aren't praying hard enough are the worst kind of people. This is a dangerous misconception. It is wrong because they are making us develop hatred for God. We then think that we are doing everything our pastor said but God is still not coming through for us because he either hates us or wants us to suffer. When we put all our trust in what the pastor says and believe and trust them more than we do God, we become deaf to what God says. We ought to know God for ourselves; being prayed for is amazing, but we shouldn't have more faith in the person praying for us than we have faith in God. You need to have a personal relationship with God. Yes, the pastors are there to help us, but their word is not what we should hold onto; we hold onto the word of God. They are human just like us, so depending on them with the magnitude that we do creates room for disappointments. They shepherd us, but they are not to be worshipped.

God made it clear to Jeremiah that he was not supposed to marry, but he wanted what he wanted and watching the woman he loved killed in his face was painful. This is a lesson for us today. When we keep holding onto something that the Lord had told us to let go of, sometimes it is taken away from us in a painful way. Maybe if we had listened and left it while we could still, we could have saved ourselves from the pain. That is when you will find a person saying that the Lord is choosy in whom he blesses, and he hates me. I have done everything; I have prayed 10 times a day, but he still didn't hear me. No one has ever told us that maybe we could have been praying the wrong prayer. Instead of approaching God to seek what He wants, we would rather dictate what we want for ourselves and expect God to perform some magic trick to make it happen exactly the way we would have preferred. When you have a desire, ask yourself whether you are going to God with it to hear what He says or if you are going with it to Him so that He can fulfill it. People often cling to the parts of scripture that only resonate with what they want; we often say in prayer, "Lord you said that "Delight yourself in the Lord and He will give you the desires of your heart; here I am Lord praying four times a day and you still are not fulfilling my desires." We skip the very first part of the scripture and run to the end because that is what suits us. Why don't we ask first what delighting ourselves in the Lord means? The original Hebrew word for delight is Asti. It demands us to find enjoyment in the Lord. He wants us to incline our hearts toward Him. Delighting in the Lord causes us to remove our focus on what we want for ourselves and to Long for what God desires as David says in the book of Psalms,

- Delight yourself in the LORD (37:4)
- Commit your way to Him (37:5)
- Rest in, and wait patiently for, The Lord (37:7)

So, before you go to God pleading with Him to do his part, first ask yourself if you have done your part.

What hurts us most as Christians is how we think that being a child of God means that we can call on God, the same way we can call out a genie and tell God what we want and then He delivers. We were told that God is our blessing ATM machine, ready to give us what we want as long as we ask. We say, "Lord, you said if your child asks for bread, you won't give him a stone, you said; seek and you will find so where are you Lord" We must shift our eyes from our current circumstances and fix them on the Lord. "I will look to the hills where my help comes from" Psalms 121: 1-2. When you delight in the Lord, you will come to realize that everything about Him is the answer to your longings. Everything God does is so that His glory may be seen. We may not understand now what He is doing in our lives but give it time and look back; you will see Him there. Listen to the song "The story I'll tell" by Naomi Raine. It explains how you may not see what God is doing now in the ruins of your life and where what is going on will lead, but we know that down through the years, we will look back at this moment and know that God was here. So, like me, at that time when all hell was breaking loose, becoming a teen mum and being shunned by everyone, the Lord was there. In the midst of all that, he was there. If I had been married to Frank at that time, there is no way I would have been where I am now and God knew this. Don't think He wasn't hurting when I was crying, The Lord feels compassion for us, but He knew he would need to not grant my request to be married to Frank because he was planning my future and Frank's part in my life had been complete. We are now totally worlds apart and when I look at us today, I fail to understand how it is that we actually even dated and that at one point I tied myself in his house. At the time when things are happening, we don't see what God is doing. We only look at the situation negatively. I could have thought that maybe God is protecting me from this man and He is trying to stop me from making the worst mistake of my life or that God is saying this isn't my portion. But we want what we want, not knowing why that door was closed. I learnt very late in my life that when God shuts a door, do not try to open it. It is for your own good.

Chapter - 3

The Widow of Zarephath Season of My Life.

"Surely God is my help; the Lord is the one who sustains me."

Psalms 54:4

"Stop running Tina. Are you crazy? The pregnancy is on you, so it makes no sense for you to flee because you have seen the delivery room sign." Shaima said, both in dismay and terror. He didn't understand why I had just bolted from the delivery room like that. Okay, let me take you back to 2 hours before.

It was a chilli day, and the fact that it was Monday didn't make it any better. I hated Mondays; I certainly didn't know this one would be special. Take another tiny piece of that clay and give it to me, I whispered to Eve as I wiped my very white and cracked lips using the heel of my palm. I had to make sure she hid it because Gogo had said that I was eating too much clay and it wasn't good for the baby. It was my biggest pregnancy craving; I had the pica disorder that compelled me to eat clay every chance I could get. Someone had said it was because I had an iron deficiency; I didn't care, I just knew that it was my favourite thing to eat. "What is it, are you okay?" Eve jumped in a panic to see why I had let out a scream that loud. "I felt a sharp excruciating pain below my belly button and then I pee'd myself," I said this with my legs spread apart, eyes wide open and my neck bent as low as it could from the side, trying to find a way to see below my gigantic belly. "That's not pee," Tanya said, "No one has that much pee," she protested. She called out for Gogo who came running. She told me that my water had broke and I was supposed to be taken to the hospital immediately. This was the moment of truth. Eve took me to the hospital and as soon as she left, I came back home running. Gogo was surprised to see me and asked why I had returned. "I don't feel any pain; it's pointless for me to stay in that hospital when I am not in labour." I arrogantly said. "Shut up and go back," she said sternly. At that moment, I felt a stabbing pain like a sharp knife had pierced me. I have never experienced such pain! It got worse; it was as though a blunt saw was cutting my insides. Gogo then called Shaima, my brother to rush with a taxi or to find a friend with a car. As we waited, I was slapping my thigh, screaming, ragging about how I was going to die and rolling on the floor. Everyone was laughing so hard. I was so dramatic about the pain; I too joined them to laugh. Shaima came with his friend and took me to the maternity ward. As we got out of the car and walked towards the ward, I saw a sign written labour ward, and I ran for my life. I ran so fast everyone thought I had lost my mind. My brother came to get me while he was laughing at me the whole time. "Get in; stop this drama, he said." I obliged and decided to be a boss about it. So, I went into the ward, found a bed, hopped on, and opened my legs as wide as I could. I Had read an article in a magazine that said when you feel the baby coming, hold your ankles and push as hard as you could. In my presumptuous foolishness and forwardness, I bent my knees and clasped my ankles and started to push. "Nurse, nurse, she is delivering the baby herself; come running," someone shouted and said with a great level of panic in their voice. Meanwhile, the 4 people who had escorted me were standing right there in front of me as I became my own midwife. Three nurses and a doctor came running, asking me to stop pushing or I would hurt the baby. "You stupid girl, what are you doing? Who told you to do that, stop pushing or you will squash the baby's head" one nurse said angrily. "Oh, oh…, I thought to myself. It is at this moment that I realized how grave the situation must have been. One doctor brought forceps and then they helped to deliver the baby. When they were done, they wrapped the bloody and pink baby in a blue sheet and handed her to me. Wow! I was dumbfounded. I had brought a whole human being into the world. I didn't know what to do. Should I scream? Should I get off the bed and jump? I was clueless. I looked at my tiny baby, and as I took her from the nurse and brought her closer to my bosom, she didn't cry; she just stared at me as if she saw right through to my soul. I whimpered and said, "Hello Chikomborero, you are finally here." It was as though time stopped ticking; my world became still, my ears grew muffled, and my heart seemed to have swelled inside my chest into a big love heart that was red and beating fast. So, this was love? My zone-out was interrupted by a wail. She cried, my baby cried; she had a voice and she cried. I cried too and to this day, that moment was the best few seconds of my life. "Don't put the black stuff on her toes; she will get ruined," I said as they tapped her feet with a black powder. The nurse put her on the scale and smiled before saying, "Baby Chicco weighs 2.7 kgs. Well done Mai Chicco for giving birth to such a healthy baby girl." I felt proud. My perspective on life changed on that June evening of 2009.

We got discharged the following day and went back home with my baby. She grew well considering her mother almost squashed her brains out. My mum would ask someone to put a chair for her outside and she would wash her granddaughter's towel-textured nappies while sitting. She did everything she could manage in her condition. We couldn't afford diapers, so she wore the white napkins that were held together by a nappy pin. Everyone helped me with her; I never felt alone or overwhelmed. I had an entire village that loved and adored my baby. (See insert for a picture of young me with baby Chicco.

When my baby was now 9 months old, I knew I had to look for a job for me to be able to fend for my child. Her father had come to apologize to my grandparents for abandoning us and was now helping to take care of the baby. My brother would help too, but I knew I didn't want to live on handouts. I had a new responsibility and I needed to step up. I began looking for a job but getting employed in a small town was close to impossible. One day as I was sitting, I heard the name Gweru in my head. I thought it was just random because, at that stage in my life, I didn't know about my gift. I just felt an inclination towards Gweru and so I went to my mother and said, "Mama, I got a job in Gweru. They said I can start on Thursday next week. Do you know anyone who lives there that can house me for a month while I work then when I get paid, I will find a room to rent on my own?" She told me that she had a long- lost friend who lived there, so we looked up her phone number in the yellow paper directory. She called her and she said I could go and stay with her daughter as she had to go to South Africa the following day. I was happy but new stress arose. I didn't have a job, so what was I going to do? Somehow, I had peace inside of me, as if someone had told me that it was going to be okay. As if there was reassurance. It was so intense to the point where I even knew that my transport would be covered. I didn't tell anyone this. The day for me to go came, but my mother had no money to give me for the trip. She asked what I was going to do. I kneeled in the living room where my grandparents and mum were sitting. "Grandpa, grandma, and mum, I am asking you to please take care of my baby for the next couple of months while I go to Gweru to start my new job. I will be sending money for her upkeep." I respectfully asked. They agreed and I said goodbye to my daughter with tears in my eyes. (See picture in insert of 9-month-old Chicco and Gogo the day I left home) I didn't tell them that I didn't have bus fare because I knew they would have been stressed so I lied and said I had the $5.

Gogo and Chicco on the day I left for Gweru.

I went to the bus station with a hobo bag that my mother had given me. It had all the clothes I owned which were still not more than 10. I didn't have even a dollar on me. I observed the bus drivers and conductors to see who amongst them had an easily approachable kind face. "Hi, my brother, how are you? I heard you calling on people announcing that you were going to Gweru. May you carry me too? I don't have money for the  fare, but I can sit on the engine of your minibus, please," I politely and sincerely asked. He said it was okay to sit on a normal seat and that he understood. We travelled well to

Gweru and when everyone was out of the minibus, the conductor worryingly said to me, "Do you know exactly where you are going, I know you said Mkoba so we can drop you off there, but I'm wondering if you know the actual address because I cannot leave you on the road at this time of the night." I told him that I didn't know but gave him Tafadzwa's phone number, the girl I was going to live with. He called her and they waited with me until she arrived. I thanked them for their kindness and thanked God for journey mercies.

I told Tafadzwa that I was going to start work the following week but also that I needed to be going into town every day to get familiar with the city. She gave me $5 for transport. I had to use this money wisely, so I went into town and took a dollar to have a CV done. I went to the SDA church that was close by and when it was time for announcements, I asked them to announce in the church that there was a lady looking for a job. After the service, one man approached me and told me that there was a boutique named Style Zone that was recruiting and gave me the directions. Monday morning, I went to that boutique with my single paged resume that had a few lines written and asked to speak to the manager. "I'm terribly sorry, but there are no longer any spots. You can try again in a few months," the manager said to me. My face dropped and as I walked out of the office, a man who had overheard our conversation said, "Oh you look really sad, I am sorry you couldn't get a job here, but I know that the casino is recruiting." My face lightened up and then I realized I had never heard of a casino so I couldn't get a job and then my face dropped once again. I was tempted to just go back home but that still voice once again reassured me. I followed the directions and went into the casino. I walked in and it was like nothing I had ever seen before. It was as though I had stepped into a playground of neon and strobing lights, there were dark brown and black tables that had wheels with numbers and some had cards on them. I remembered seeing these in an Ocean's Eleven movie. The ambience was captivating. I cluelessly walked toward something that looked like a cashier's desk. As I passed through the swishing automatic doors and heard the crank of slot machines and the clink of coins, alarms announcing winners,

I couldn't help but wonder if I even had the capacity to understand any of the things that were surrounding me. You see, I came from a very small town that had one set of traffic lights. I had never been into anything remotely close to the sophisticated place I had just walked into. "Can I help you with something?" a man in a well-ironed black suit asked in an annoyed tone. "I, I am looking for the manager," I murmured. He frowned and pointed me toward an office. I knocked and a male voice said to come in. I clumsily walked in, I looked ridiculous, and I didn't even know what to say to this man. He looked at me in a way that said, "So, talk." My voice quavered as I said, "I am looking for a job," and handed him that CV. Frowning a bit, he turned over the page to see if there was anything at the back. He straightened his chair and did his best to concentrate. I imagined he was going to call security to have them remove the ratchet girl that was now just standing at the other side of his expensive desk. "What job are you looking for, this cv simply says what subjects you did in high school and nothing else." He spoke. "I am looking for any job, whatever it is that you do here, I can learn fast. If not, I can also clean very well so even a cleaning job will do." Now he was annoyed and said, "Any vacancies that Regency Casino may have are posted in the national newspaper, the Herald. You can buy one of those and apply. The people that you see there applied at our head office in Harare and went to be interviewed twice. Like I said, buy the press next year and apply for the croupier position." I wanted to slap myself silly. Did I think I would have been given any type of job here? I swallowed hard and thanked him for his time and walked out of his office. Embarrassment washed over me. There was poverty written all over me and I had had the guts to speak to this man who looked like he came from money. As those fancy automatic doors opened again to let me out, I heard that man's voice saying, "Tina, come back in here." I froze. He called me by my name. I went back into his office, and he shut the door behind him and then sighed heavily and said, "Urgh! I don't know what I am doing, but I will do it anyway. So, there was something about you that is compelling me to give you a job. I don't know what it is, but as soon as you walked out of that door, I knew I had to give you this job. I will probably get fired for this because I have broken protocol in every way but tomorrow morning, I need you to come back here wearing a white shirt and black pants. You are joining my training class to become a croupier." I opened my mouth and said nothing. I couldn't believe my ears. The fist of despair that gripped me loosened. My prayer was answered. But wait, I hadn't prayed for this, but God just came through just like that? It was at that moment that I realized miracles are real. I began to shake as I said thank you. I wanted to kneel and thank him. I saw his eyes clouding with tears as I repeatedly thanked him over and over.

I went back home running. I jumped at Tafadzwa screaming with joy. I was just so elated. She asked me to calm down and tell her what had happened, and I told her. "No, no," she said with a smile on her face. "No one gets a job at that casino. Let me tell you. Since it opened, everyone has been dying to work there; most people that I know failed the interview in Harare and you are saying you went to town for a few hours and came back with a job there?" She couldn't believe it. I didn't have the clothes I was told to come wearing and she didn't either, so she went to ask her friend down the road who then agreed to lend me her black pants and old school shirt. I went to work the following day; I had only one dollar left. I didn't know where I was going to find money to return home. Farai was the name of my new manager. Yes, that Rimuka girl had a manager now. Farai told his best trainee to teach me everything they had done so far. She hated me and told me that point blank. She said they had to go for two interviews and had to wait months to get a job while I waltzed in yesterday and got one. She spoke about how it wasn't fair and how a person of my calibre wouldn't master all the casino games. She trained me harshly, not knowing I had survived worse. After the training, Farai called me back into his office. Everyone had left. "Tina, I couldn't sleep last night thinking about you, about how you ended up here. Tell me your story." He asked. I told him exactly how I had gotten there and that I somehow knew there was a job there for me. He smiled. I suspect he was a Godly man because telling him my story somehow put him at ease. He then called someone else to join us and he went on to say, "Tina, I am going to do something else for you, but make sure you don't tell anyone or else we would both lose our jobs. So, Samson and I are managers, he is a pit boss, and we live in the company residence that is specifically for managers only. No trainee can ever live there but we have an extra room and so we are going to take you in." Again, I froze. Was all this really happening? I couldn't fathom any of this. He then handed me a $10 bill and said to go and take my belongings from Tafadzwa's house and bring them to their place. Again, Tafadzwa didn't believe this. It was all happening so fast. Within 4 days, I had gone to a town I had never set foot in, found a job, and found a luxurious place to stay in the suburbs. Wow, it can only be God. When we got to the house, they showed me my room and the two men became my brothers. I would cook and clean for them. I wasn't getting paid during the training for 3 months, but they took care of me. Helped with transport money and bought me food. They were kind to me; to this day, they were the kindest people I have ever encountered. After training, I got my uniforms. I looked so good in them, and I couldn't believe it. I had changed, literally. (See pictures in insert) My first paycheck came; it was the most money that I had ever held in my hands. I bought my first cellphone and sent the rest of it home to my family. It was so much money that my grandma called and said she thought I had robbed a bank because it didn't make sense that I had gotten a job that paid me so much.

A photo of me in uniform

The God who sees. Jehovah El Roi (Genesis 16:13)

1 Kings 17:7 -16." Then the word of the LORD came to Elijah: 9 "Go at once to Zarephath in the region of Sidon and stay there. I have directed a widow there to supply you with food."

10 So he went to Zarephath. When he came to the town gate, a widow was there gathering sticks. He called to her and asked, "Would you bring me a little water in a jar so I may have a drink?" 11 As she was going to get it, he called, "And bring me, please, a piece of bread."

¹² "As surely as the LORD your God lives," she replied, "I don't have any bread—only a handful of flour in a jar and a little olive oil in a jug. I am gathering a few sticks to take home and make a meal for myself and my son, that we may eat it—and die."

¹³ Elijah said to her, "Don't be afraid. Go home and do as you have said. But first make a small loaf of bread for me from what you have and bring it to me, and then make something for yourself and your son. ¹⁴ For this is what the LORD, the God of Israel, says: 'The jar of flour will not be used up and the jug of oil will not run dry until the day the LORD sends rain on the land.'"

Just as the Lord thought about this widow in Zarephath when Elijah was miles away, the Lord thought about me when I was in a different town and led me to a place where I was going to encounter Him as Jehovah Jireh, the Provider. This is a life lesson of God's supernatural provision. When the Lord wants to show you that it is Him doing a thing in your life, He will do it in a way that no man could ever do. He will do it with such intricate finesse that even you would be unable to comprehend. Let's take a look again at how I ended up in Gweru and how things all unfolded in my favour. I met destiny helpers along the way, and it didn't stop there. It was all mapped out to show His divine favour upon my life. I called this the Widow of Zarephath chapter because the widow was a single mother, as I was. Just like me, she was in a town where there was drought and the Lord's grace located her and singled her out to qualify for a miracle. Her food provision had run out for her and her child, we don't have the full story, but we can assume that the little food that she had left, her relatives or friends had given her, and she couldn't keep going back for more. And at a time when the Lord knew she wouldn't have enough for tomorrow, the Lord whispered in her ear and said," Go and fetch firewood." Elijah met her when she had gotten out of her home in pursuit of something, the same way I met Farai after the Lord had whispered in my ear to say, "Go to Gweru."

Bear in mind this widow knew she didn't have food to make with this firewood but that didn't stop her from going to find the firewood anyway because she knew that one word from God was enough. She knew that all she had to do was listen and take the first step; the rest the Lord would provide. This is also what happened to me. I just knew that if the Lord had told me to go to Gweru, he would also provide the means for me to get there. You see, God does not require our help to map out a plan for our lives, He requires only our trust. He is the God who sees. All we need to do is take the first step and the rest will fall into place. It could be the Lord has put something in your heart and you are afraid to begin because you do not know how it will end. But remember that 19-year-old girl who just heard the word Gweru and she obeyed without knowing what was in store when she got there. Take the first step; you do not need to see the whole staircase. The Lord speaks to each of us differently; deep inside, you have heard Him speak, but you may be ignoring Him. That still resilient voice that told you No, that feeling that you like to call your sixth sense, that dream you keep shoving aside, go back to it and hear what the Lord is saying to you. What the Lord is telling you to do, where He is telling you to go, what He is telling you to look at. In faith, the Widow gave all of her last food to Elijah. In faith, I used the last dollar I had to go and look for a job. That leap of faith opened God's provision. The widow kept getting her jars of flour and oil filled with more than enough every day, just as I got a salary that was way more than enough to sustain me and my daughter for years to come. I know that you could be praying every day for the Lord to provide; we call on Him and "say Jehovah Jireh, you provided a lamb for Abraham, why won't you provide for me too, Lord you said ask "and it shall be given to you but how come you aren't giving me anything that I ask for." Pause for a minute and see; Abraham listened to God's voice when He said "Go" to the altar. He had to oblige first before a miraculous provision was put before him. He took his first step; have you taken your first step? Are you asking the Lord to meet you while you are still sitting in your comfort zone? Remember, to meet someone; you have to be going somewhere; you have to first embark on a journey. Go wherever the Lord is leading you even if you don't know how you will get there, He will meet you on the way and provide for you. Everyone I wrote about in this chapter met God when they were told to Go. Just Go.

Chapter - 4

The Rahab Season of My Life

"For none of us are where we are without leaving where we were."

(Unknown)

"How many rooms is the house and how much would we be paying the maid?" Ba Fay asked while holding my hand in a way a man who is about to leave his daughter in boarding school would. I heard him but my mind was elsewhere, so I didn't respond. He probably thought I was mad about something, so he gently tilted my chin toward his face and smiled as he said, "Don't stress; we can afford it, Tina." I believed him, but I wasn't stressed because of that. I was busy figuring out whom I'd introduce him as to my daughter. He certainly wasn't my boyfriend, and he wasn't my relative either. Was this a wise decision? Well, even if it wasn't, it was now too late to turn back. I bumped into Ba Fay a month ago when I went to Kadoma to visit my family. He was no stranger to me; he was one of my father's wealthy clients. He used to come to the shop when I was the receptionist. He had heard about my dad leaving us, just like the entire city had. He felt sad for me. He looked at me differently compared to the past. You see, I was much older now; I wasn't that teenager that he knew. Of course, he was attracted to me; my body had developed into a full figure, and it now looked like that of my mother's. I was no longer that tiny scrawny girl; I was now well endowed, with a curvy body that was quite buxom. I knew he was infatuated and so I used that to my advantage to ensnare him. I had decided to leave the casino because I couldn't live with Chicco while I worked there, so I wanted a job that would allow me to be with my child every day. Ba Fay had offered a great opportunity. He had asked if I was able to complete college and when I said no, he offered to take me back to school. "I don't want you to feel that my taking you back to school was so that I could exploit you, no. There are no strings attached to my gesture. I know you are an intelligent girl who never got the chance to complete school, so I am going to pay for rent, a maid, Chicco's Montessori fees and take care of everything." I respected him for separating his feelings towards me and what he intended to do for me. I began living in Harare under the care of this man. He didn't want me to lack anything, so he would make sure he gave us a lot of money every Friday. It was more than I earned at the casino, so it's safe to say we were living a lavish life. As I made new friends, societal pressure began to kick in. I now had this insistence to get married because everyone around me kept telling me that some single mothers were getting married, and I was no different from them. In my pursuit to find a man to marry, I went through a lot of heartbreaks. I pushed some relationships that were not worth it and when that didn't work, I began creating a wall around myself. I decided that I would flee from a man as soon as I began seeing signs of possible heartbreak. I experienced bouts of confusion during this stage of my life. I kept being bombarded by people saying, "A woman like you isn't married; something must be wrong with you." It was said so much that I began to believe that something was wrong with me. I then made friends that told me they knew people who could remove the "bad luck" that was lingering around me. So, I believed them and began finding people who could "remove" the bad luck. One day, I and my friends Tanya & Rumbi went to a different town in Bindura to meet a sorcerer who claimed he could rid us of the evil spirits that were hindering us from getting married. When we got in, this man said, "Eeee vekwa Butau." I smiled and thought that if this man knew my surname before he even looked at my face, then I must be in the right place. When we got in, he said he saw us while we were still on the way. He told us all the same thing, phrased differently. He basically said we all weren't married because we had spiritual husbands. He said we needed to come back a week later after he got back from Malawi so that he could cleanse us. So, we left without getting anything done or given to us; he just told us to come back in a week and asked us to leave; we left happily with the hopes that all our problems would disappear after we come back. On our way back to Harare, I received a call from Chicco's grandmother's pastor, Baba Prince. As soon as I answered the phone, he frantically said, "Tina what are you doing going to a place like that? God gave me a vision where I saw you going to Bindura and He told me to pray for you at once. So, before you get to your house, come here and we can pray a cleansing prayer." The phone was on loudspeaker, so my friends heard this and panicked. They asked to join me to go to the pastor. Once we got there, he said that we had gone into a dangerous place and that we should thank God for coming to our rescue. He prayed for us and told us to pray ourselves asking God to forgive us. I went home and did as I was instructed. After that incident, it became very clear that God loved me and was there for me. I had forgotten where He took me from because I was now living this lavish ungodly life. I then began seeking the Lord, and a particular song made me realize just how much His mercy had rescued me from the darkness. It is a song by the Acapella Company called: Rescue.

> *It says, "Lord You know everything I've*
> *done Every thought I've had, You*
> *know everyone And Lord You*
> *know every time I fall*
> *Still, You come to my rescue when I call*
> *Lord, You hear every idle word*
> *Every thoughtless deed, how it seems*
> *absurd That Lord You give, not*
> *what I am due But mercy; You come*
> *to my rescue"*

I can safely say that this was the stage in my life when I knew that the Lord leads me. I was about to get myself into things I didn't know due to the pressure of getting married. I had forgotten where the Lord took me from and had gone back to trying to figure it out by myself. His love and patience with me drew me back to Him. He came to my rescue when I had almost put myself in trouble. I began to pray, and my spiritual muscle began to slowly develop. I joined a group of prayerful ladies along with my cousin Theresa, to go to the prayer mountain called Mutemwa in Mutoko. We had heard so many wonderful things regarding how the mountain was holy ground. We went there and were instructed on how to pray the Novena prayer before we climbed into the mountain. It was a very steep and difficult climb, but we made it to the top. You may assume that I prayed for a husband, but No. I prayed only for my child the entire night. I had come to understand that when the time was right, the Lord would make the marriage happen. I prayed that my child would be spared from any generational curses and that she would become a God-fearing woman. I covered my child immensely during that all-night prayer. I learnt a lot about Novena Prayers. Some of the ladies in the mountain had so many testimonies from those prayers.

At this point, it felt wrong for me to still be with Ba Fay because our relationship had progressed. I told him that I needed to let him go and that I wanted to work for my daughter and take care of her with my own hard-earned money. I didn't want to be a kept woman anymore. He was heartbroken, but I had to follow the Lord's path. To become a follower of Christ, I needed to dump everything I knew and follow him. I then changed locations and moved to a part of Harare that he didn't know and there I made new friends. Of the friends that I made, one was put in my life so that she would walk this spiritual journey with me. We were very unlikely friends but somehow, we clicked and began living together. Her name is Kudzai. Kudzai began engaging me in prayer each night. I felt that she was overdoing it because then I was still very young spiritually, she was way more advanced than I was and so I judged her, thinking that she was "holier" than others. Oh, how very lost I was. Some nights, I wouldn't join her in prayer and some I would roll my eyes thinking here we go again. I judged her because I didn't understand what she was experiencing and didn't know that simply because I had never encountered something didn't mean it wasn't real or of God. She would pray in tongues and sometimes would fall to the ground; I honestly thought she was being dramatic because I wasn't there yet spiritually. She would say things that I thought were weird like, "The Lord showed me this." I would roll my eyes, telling myself that she thinks God can talk to her. She must be delusional. What did I know? Our friendship grew into a sisterhood. We began doing everything together; we would go to Kadoma to visit my family together. Late at night, I would tell her stories of my escapades and we would laugh for hours. One day, Kudzai and I went to do a charity run in Epworth. Kudzai does charity work. While we were there to give a disabled girl food, the girl's mother turned to me and said, "You, the Lord has shown me something about your future. I saw you getting married to a man that loves you incredibly. I saw you sitting in an aeroplane going to a country that is far. It is a country that I have never heard of, but I can see that it is not the UK. You spent hours and hours on that plane and when you got there, you met a man that loved you." I was stunned. She just gave me this prophecy out of nowhere. We went back home and laughed with Kudzai because I thought to myself, the only family that I have out of Zimbabwe is in England, so if I ever leave my home country, it would be to go to the UK. We dismissed the prophecy and forgot all about it.

A year later, things became very hard for me in Harare. I had lost my job at Zesa and had no income. I felt a strong urge to go to a different country to find employment. So, I went to Dubai with the help of my aunt. When I got to Dubai, I worked for a plastic surgeon. One day she saw me wearing body-hugging clothes and fired me, so I had to find another job, no matter what it was. I cook well, so I looked for a job as a cook and I was hired by a family that wanted a personal chef who could also clean. I do both very well, so I took the job. One day I cooked and my boss' husband and her father-in-law commended my cooking so much that she was annoyed and fired me. She said that her husband had never said to her all those words he had said to me and that made her uncomfortable. That night that I was fired, I went into the park to take a walk and to pray. I felt that the Lord was dealing me a losing hand. I was fired for silly things twice in the space of a few months. When I was praying, I heard myself say, "Lord please pave my way to Canada; when I get there may everything be as you will it to be." I panicked and sat down. I didn't know the words that had just come out of my mouth. I hadn't said them willingly; it was as though someone else within me had spoken those words. I brushed it off. That night as I was scrolling through Facebook, one man named Brian commented and said something that got my attention. He was telling a lady that had a problem she had shared that God allows for certain things to happen because it is our path and we had to pass through it. I sent him a message in his inbox asking him to shed more light and he asked to do a Skype call. A few minutes into the teaching, Brian said, "Tina, the Lord has told me to tell you that you have a special gift. You are able to see things spiritually in your life as they happen or before they do and also things about the people around you. Lastly, you are a prayer warrior; by that I mean you can pray for others and set them free from different spiritual bondages and pray over their situations to change." I wanted to slap this guy; he was saying nonsense. I was just a woman trying to find God and desperately trying to live right, this was just now drama to me. I was enraged & I thought to myself, "here we go again." Why do these strange people keep coming at me with prophecies that aren't even real. He sounded deranged to me, and I didn't have time for his games. I just thought he would teach me about the Lord. I said thank you and never spoke to him again. In fact, I deleted his number from my phone and Skype. What he was saying didn't make sense and I knew that I wasn't capable of any of the things he had described about me. I didn't tell anyone, not even Kudzai because I thought that was absurd. I went back home to Zimbabwe to try and find something else to do. I applied for a visa to go to the UK, and I was denied; a friend told me about the Netherlands, and I was denied; I tried the US visa and was denied, then lastly a Schengen visa and I was denied too. I lost hope and almost went back to Ba Fay to say that I wanted to be a kept woman again but then, God walked in once again and He changed my life forever.

*"Therefore, since we are surrounded by such a huge crowd
of witnesses to the life of faith, let us strip off every weight that
slows us down, especially the sin that so easily trips us up.
And let us run with endurance the
race God has set before us.*

"Hebrews 12:1

God Chooses the Most Unlikely People
(Judges 6:15)

One thing that is consistent about God, even in the bible is that He uses unlikely people. He takes the ones that are deemed unworthy by society and everyone around them and calls them to do His work. Gideon was the least in his father's house (possibly what we call the black sheep of the family) Paul was murdering God's people before He was called. David whom the bible said was a man after God's own heart was an adulterer. When Jesus chose his disciples, He didn't choose the perfect men in society; he chose the broken ones. He even chose Judas and God is omnipresent, He knew that Judas would betray Him but still gave him a chance. He knew Peter would deny Him, but he chose him anyway. What this means is that the Lord gives each one of us a chance for redemption.

God uses unexpected people in imperfect situations to accomplish His perfect will.

Our focus in this Chapter is Rahab (Joshua 2: 1-24) who had heard about the Lord that had parted the red sea and longed to encounter Him. She knew that if He had changed the lives of the Israelites miraculously, He could change her life too. She put faith that God would usher her into new beginnings. Who knew that the repulsive Rahab would one day be in the lineage of our Lord and Saviour Jesus Christ? I too was lost, and the Lord sent someone to find me. I wanted to now encounter this God that had the power to send someone to rescue me from a snare that I had created for myself.

Society is our greatest enemy. It tells us how we are less if we are single mothers. It shuns us one way or the other. In the church, single mothers do not have space, they don't qualify for the youth group anymore, and they certainly aren't allowed in the women's fellowship either because, in that group, the women are praying for their husbands, praying for their marriages. Yes, you could go, but would you be accepted? Do they talk about the burdens you face? Certainly not. So, single mothers end up not being involved in any church groups or ultimately stop going to church altogether. The stigma behind being called a single mother leaves these women feeling like they don't belong anywhere.

Validation of Single Mums

I want to talk to single mums. You are enough and yes, God can use you the same way He is using me (read the chapters that follow for how God made me his unlikely vessel) because to Him, you are a perfect imperfection. Do not be pressured into getting married so that you can fit in. You are strong, you are doing the job of 2 parents by yourself, and you are being a boss about it. Yes, sometimes it gets hard, cry, but pick yourself up and keep going because you are all your baby/babies have. They stopped inviting you to their functions. Well, that's ok too; find other women that are in a similar season with you and create your own functions. Stop wallowing in self-pity. Anyone that tells you that your singleness is a curse has no idea what they are talking about. Life has seasons and God sometimes allows you to be single so that you can find yourself. Fall in love with who you are. Singleness is a state to be pursued, not avoided. In singleness, you discover yourself, you find the things that make you unique and it is the only time that you can be whole and complete. We were told that marriage completes us, but this isn't true. You need to be complete and whole to offer value to your husband. Finding yourself means that you will need time alone and sometimes we don't recognize this as a blessing. Society says you are not enough when you are unmarried, but you need to be whole first before you are married so that you are not a burden to your spouse. You will then start seeking validation from your partner because you don't know what you are worth. Find your worth in your singleness and discover yourself. Be complete by yourself so that you are somebody that doesn't need their value to be determined by the next person. Some of the loneliest people in the world are married people because marriage doesn't get rid of loneliness; it just exposes it. We think that marriage will remove the loneliest in our hearts, so we get desperate for it. If you are lonely single, you will also be lonely married, so the goal is to find yourself because just like all the things in life, there is a season for everything, so make the most out of your lonely season so that you may be a good spouse in your married season. We prepare the ground first before the sowing begins and we sow and wait for the rain. What would happen if we do not prepare the ground first? Can you sow in the midst of weeds and thorns? Ground preparation is necessary for a great harvest; we take time to prepare for it, so why aren't we taking time to prepare ourselves for marriage by falling in love with ourselves and being whole alone? You are not going to be happy with someone else if you are not happy by yourself. You will get frustrated when your spouse doesn't complete you. No human can meet your soul needs; only you can do that, so maybe the Lord has allowed you to be single so you can find yourself and reconnect with your being.

So that takes me to the issue of pressure. The shame of being unmarried gave my friend and me pressure to try and rid ourselves of the one thing that we thought was standing in our way of marriage. We were willing to go high and low just so that we could fit in. The Lord let me experience this so that I could teach it from experience. Sometimes, the Lord lets someone go through something for them to fully understand it if they are going to be tasked to teach about it. For example, I needed to write this book while I was still in my singleness season because I am experiencing it and can relate. Just as a single mom won't likely be invited to teach about the different roles in marriage, anyone else who isn't a single mother cannot speak about the hardships single mums face. They can try, but without experience, they may not be able to articulate it well.

From my experience, do not let anything or anyone tell you that there is something wrong with you being single. It is a season, so no matter what you do, if it isn't time for the season to end, it will not end. You cannot pray yourself out of a season. No sorcerer can take you out of a season.

Let us use the example of an Apple tree. An apple tree takes an average of 5 years to grow fruit. Even if you water it every day and put fertilizer, when the 5 years are not up, it will never grow fruit because it isn't time and season yet. So just like you, you may be told that you are still single because you aren't praying enough or fasting enough. Others will tell you that this type of singleness needs you to go to a sorcerer. Do not do it. Not everyone will be as fortunate as I was to have God send someone to tell me how dangerous the step I had taken was. All sorcery comes with a price; if I had gone back to that Bindura man, who knows what would have happened? Some of the problems that we now call generational curses are things that our mothers/fathers got for themselves when they went to a sorcerer to try and fix a problem. Just like us, we may be given a quick fix but then our children pay the price or worse, we could get initiated into satanism and cults without realizing it. In taking their "portions" that promise to eradicate all your problems, you may be bringing problems that you will not be able to deal with. What usually happens is that when we find ourselves suffering from the things that we would have gone to find on our own, we now want to turn to God to ask Him to help us when it is already too late. There is a Facebook group for women who confess about the things they were given by sorcerers that turned on them and became goblins or worse. They sacrifice themselves and their families because all sorcery comes with a price. Some of them write their stories on their death bed to try and warn. Instead of seeking fortune tellers and sorcerers, let us ask why God chose this time to be your season of singleness. You may find that in that season, you will grow and become in touch with yourself more than in any other season of your life. I had to experience what I experienced so that I would know and understand the darkness of this world. I had my very close friend who reminded me of what I told her over 8 years ago. She was stressed about not getting married and she had been given a name of a sorcerer who could help her. She came to me and told me, and she reminded me that when I stopped her, I said, "You don't have to go to a fortune teller/ sorcerer. I have done that already for both of us; I have sinned already for both of us, so there is no need for you to go." I was in awe of my response. It then teaches us that sometimes, someone who has already walked a certain path is qualified to give you advice because they have been there before. We need to listen to the people who love us and who are around us when they hold us back from doing something wrong. May my experience stop you from seeking other things or people that aren't God simply because you think your season is now.

Chapter - 5

The Israelites Season of My Life

"For we are God's masterpiece. He has created us anew in Christ Jesus, so we can do the things He planned for us long ago."

Ephesians 2:10

"Kudzai, if I am denied this visa, I am going to leave this Godly path and just return to my old ways. I'm trying to change, to be good and it seems all my attempts are in vain." I said in a sad voice. My friend didn't answer; I simply heard her praying to the Lord saying that she didn't know what to do with me. She finished and we went to sleep. The following day, we took the paperwork that was in the khaki envelope. We prayed over it and began to walk to the VFS center where we were going to submit it. This time, I hadn't told anyone that I was going to apply for this visa. We held hands and walked while we spoke about other things. We submitted the visa application, and I went to Kadoma because we had been told that the process would take between 6 – 8 weeks. I was broke now and I planned to wait out the 6 or so weeks at home with my grandma and mother. Kudzai didn't go with me because I was going to be home for a very long time.

On Thursday morning, there was no electricity, so my grandmother and I were cooking outside. We had a spot that was behind the house, beneath the clothesline, that we reserved for cooking with firewood. The sun was scorching hot, and I had sweat drops all over my face; some probably trickled down and fell into the pan of fish that I was roasting. Gogo would sit with me and keep me company while I cooked every time, so having her here in the sun with me was not a new thing. We gossiped about our neighbours and talked about anything. We had a maid at the house, but my grandmother preferred my cooking, so I made sure I did so every time I could. I heard my phone ring but didn't get up to answer; then it rang again and Chicco came running with it. "Hello…, yes, this is she," I said into the phone. I must have begun shaking because I heard my grandmother asking me what was wrong. I couldn't believe this. I dropped the fork that I held onto the ground and ran to get shoes. I was so frantic that everyone around me was asking what was going on. "Gogo & Mama, I am going back to Harare now, something came up and I need to leave right this moment." The fish on the fire must have been burning but at this time, I didn't care. I hadn't bathed and I still wore my grandmother's skirt and blouse that smelled of smoke and fish and I ran to get a lift back to Harare as I was. While I waited at the hitchhiking spot at the Kadoma Ranch Hotel, I called Kudzai. "I'm on my way back right now; something has happened. I got a call from the consulate, and they said to come and collect my passport. Kudzai, it has only been 3 days, so I know this is a denial," I said in a shaky voice. She asked me to calm down and I barked at her and said, "Don't ask me to calm down; I think I'm going mad; I can't breathe, Kudzai I'm shaking. What do I do?" "Calm down Tina, get here first, then we will figure it out together. Right now, I need you to calm down and look for transport," Kudzai said in a firm voice. I obliged, but that didn't stop my body from shaking. A man driving past saw me and reversed. He said, "Sister are you okay? Is everything all right? Where are you going?" I could only answer one of his questions and said, "I'm going to Harare." He must have said let's go, I didn't hear much but I just know that when my phone rang again, I said to Kudzai I was now an hour away. So this means that we had already driven for about 45 minutes. The man was nice enough to drop me off at our apartment and Kudzai came to pick me up at the gate. We were stressed together and didn't sleep the entire night. At 5 am, she made us tea and we left the house around 9 to go again to the VFS centre on foot. "Wow, I don't know what you have done, but I have never seen a passport return so quickly in all my 5 years working here. Here you go." Said the light-skinned who stood at the other side of the desk. I simply said thank you and we grabbed the passport and ran. When we got to the traffic light, we stood in front of a car that was driving toward us and held out our hands in a stop signal. The man honked and cursed while applying his emergency brakes. It happened in a way that we see in the movies. "I'm sorry I stopped you like this; we need a lift home and now, something is going on and you must take us home," I shouted. He took us home and we literally jumped out of the car as soon as we got there, running we called out our thank you. As soon as we were inside, we tore open that plastic paper and frantically began to scroll the pages of my passport. There was nothing. We froze. Kudzai scrolled too, but we saw nothing. I could feel an ache in the lower level of my spine. I felt dizzy; I didn't know if I wanted to sit on the floor or lean on the wall. Then slowly, I opened my passport pages again and there it was, the thick yellow-like paper written CANADA boldly in red, with a metallic maple leaf on the furthermost left corner. I must have died for a few seconds because the thing that brought me to life was the piercing scream that Kudzai let out. I joined her and we screamed so loud as we jumped up and down in ecstasy. Tears of joy from both our faces spewed all over. The neighbour came running but that didn't stop us from screaming. She kept asking if we were okay, but we were just engrossed in a hug that was so tight nothing could have separated us. We remained in that tight hug as we cried together; all the neighbour could do was rub both our shoulders in an attempt to calm us down. "Sorry, we were just so happy, Tina's visa came out and we couldn't believe it," Kudzai said in the groggiest voice I have ever heard. She must have thought we were being dramatic for nothing because she didn't understand what we were going through. We were so happy. After an hour or so when we were calmer, Kudzai said we now needed to tell my family and my friends. I called my two aunties in the UK and my brother who was now living in the US.

"Hmm Tina, I don't think what you are saying is true. Getting a Canadian visa is almost impossible but getting it in 3 days is something that is unheard of. That visa takes almost 3 weeks to come out if at all it does." Shaima said. Convincing him that I had indeed been granted a 10-year visa to Canada in 3 days was going to be difficult. Even I couldn't understand the miraculous turn of events so how then would I have explained to him something that I couldn't comprehend? My aunties too weren't buying it; not to blame them; this was all too good to be true. My friend Emily was overjoyed because she had been recently married and she too was moving to Canada soon, so knowing that she was going to come when I was there meant both of us didn't need to stress about finding friends in a faraway land. I had to leave for Canada soon, and the flight prices were exorbitant, so my family pooled in the money that was needed to buy a ticket. I had to leave Chicco in boarding school under the care of my then-best friend. The ticket was bought, and I went home to Kadoma to say my goodbyes to my family.

On that Tuesday morning, my friends came to say their goodbyes. We all sat in our apartment. As the afternoon drew closer, I called my travel agent to inform them that I would pass through their office to collect my ticket. The phone rang, but there was no answer. I called again and I got the same feedback. Shaking, I dialled the number for the office that was next door to them at travel thaza. The lady on the phone informed me that the travel agent had been arrested so the office was shut. I grew numb. I think I turned pale because when I licked my lips, they were dry, and my saliva was white and frothy. I felt my eyes shoot and my vision got blurry. Everyone was panicking and asking what was wrong. I sat down and grew weaker. I felt defeated. What was I going to tell my family that had bought the ticket? What was going to happen to me? None of us had an answer. The time was now 2:15 pm and check-in was beginning in an hour. I quite simply wanted to scream. As I sat there and all of us were consumed by our different thoughts, a still small voice said a name in my ear. I heard it twice. It felt like a eureka moment for me as I jumped from the sofa I once deeply sat in and said, "Guys, I know what we should do; there is a name that was kind of whispered to my heart; the name is Simba Chakawa. I don't know who he is, but his name just came to my mind; I'm telling you; I have a feeling he is our answer." Arthur looked at me with a sharp eye and irritably said, "Tina, this is your problem. You think you can joke even in the direst of times. This isn't amusing at all; you are wasting our time." I did feel stupid for a moment, but there was a sense of reassurance in me that I could not begin to even explain. I cleared my voice and boldly said, "Guys, I know it sounds absurd, but I know what I am talking about, reach out to your contacts and start asking if anyone knows this man and find me his contact details." The seriousness in my voice got everyone jolted. One of my friends then said, "I have heard that name before; I know someone who might know this guy's number." Hope flooded the room; we all became alive again. She made a call, and the number was found and then when I had it, everyone looked at me with a look that said, "Now what?"

Straightening my posture, I dialled the number. It rang twice and then a strange "Hello" answered. I swallowed hard and said, "Hello, could I please speak to Mr. Chakawa…, my name is Tina, you do not know me and I do not know you but I just got a feeling that you may be able to help me. A few years ago, I heard your name being spoken about in a crowd of friends and today when I got into a crisis, your name is the one that came into my mind." "Yes, what can I help you with?" he inquired. "I had bought a ticket from Travel thaza, but I heard they were arrested, so I have no way to get to Canada." I continued. There was dead silence before he asked me what I needed from him. I told him that I needed whatever assistance his influence could get me, and he simply said, "Ok, send me your passport biometric page and visa," he quickly said before plainly hanging up on me without saying anything else. The phone was on loudspeaker, so everyone heard this loud ding of the other line dropping. Tension grew, but no one said a thing. I wanted to evaporate or disappear; whichever one was faster. It seemed as though the room got smaller because I could hear everyone's unsteady breathing. Even that ticking clock was making an awful lot of noise. Why did I do this crazy thing? This was beyond embarrassing. Maybe let me just accept that this is a failed trip and count my losses. I began planning how to convey the message to my family; I thought maybe I would get Kudzai to call them and explain. "Ding ding, ding ding, my phone vibrated and rang to signal a text message. I grabbed it quickly and opened the text. I couldn't believe my eyes! There was a picture of a ticket, and as I fumbled to read the details, the phone rang and Simba said, "Hi Tina, did you receive the ticket? I put you on the same flight you were supposed to take. It's 3:12 right now, check in closes in 40 minutes so rush to the airport and let me know once you get to Canada." My God! What had just happened here? My jaw dropped, tears gushed, and

Tina Butau

I must have mumbled something inaudible because he then said, "There is no time to cry; run along you will miss your flight." I felt as though I was floating; sunshine flooded my soul. Was I dreaming? This strange man that I had spoken to for barely 2 minutes had bought me a $2650 flight. So, this was what they said when they said He is a miracle-working God? Everyone was screaming with Joy, and we all went to Emily's car and sped to the airport. No one said much on the way; I'm guessing everyone was just still trying to understand what had just happened before our eyes.

We got to the airport and check-in had closed. The lady was about to leave the desk but said, "You are late; I don't know if you are going to make it on time. You are lucky I hadn't already logged out; let me check you in. Let's hope you make it." I didn't have time to hug all my friends goodbye, so I just ran with tears flowing. They were crying too; I heard it in their voices when they called my name. I quickly passed customs and managed to make it into the flight. Wow. That is all I could think of. The plane took off and I felt a sense of peace. We arrived in Dubai and the devil played a number on me. When we were in the queue to board our connecting flight, a man in a black suit just came and grabbed me into the detention centre. He simply told me I was being detained and locked me in the room without explanation. I felt terrified. I didn't know what was going on. As I sat in that room I began to pray. I desperately needed God to rescue me. I called Kudzai to let her know and was devastated. "Boarding will close in 5 minutes for Flight 502 to Toronto", a lady in the speaker announced. I began to shiver now. What was I going to do? The 5 minutes lapsed, and she announced again that boarding was closed. I began to cry now and started to pace the small room while I continued to pray. A few moments later, the same man who had detained me budged into the room in haste, grinning as he said, "I am terribly sorry; there was a misunderstanding. Give me your bag right now and run along with me." The confusion on my face made him repeat himself. He then took out his walkie-talkie and demanded for them to open the boarding gate for me in a very authoritative voice.

Thankfully, the plane door hadn't been shut yet, so I barely made it in. The flight attendant looked at my face in horror. My eyes must have been bloodshot from the crying, my face was swollen, and I was still mumbling in prayer. I don't even know what I was saying, I just remember saying "I don't know" over and over. She could see I wasn't in the right state of mind, so she grabbed the passport and boarding pass that I still had in my hand. "27 E, that is your seat number, I will take care of you, and everything will just be all right", she said as she literally pushed me to walk to my seat. As soon as I sat there, I fell fast asleep and woke up after a couple of hours. I asked for the 10-minute free Wi-Fi and texted everyone to let them know that I was 3 hours from Toronto. I arrived and all I could think of was how great The Lord is.

When I was now leaving the airport to get to the hotel that my brother had booked for me, another name came to my mind. I cannot say it was whispered to me the way Simba's name had been; it just came into my head. I remembered that the guy I had spoken to on Skype when I was still in Dubai had said that he lived in Canada. Brian was his name. I had no phone number, so I sent him a Facebook message that said, "Hi Brian, I wanted to let you know that I am in Canada now; if you are in Toronto, maybe we can meet one day."

In that instant, he replied and asked where I was. I told him that I was at the airport, and he immediately called using the same Facebook app. "Tina, you won't believe this! I was coming from work, and I just somehow lost my way home and ended up at the airport. I don't understand how I got lost; I have been using the same road for the past 14 years. Now I know what happened; I was being led to you. Which gate are you at? okay give me 4 minutes and I will be there." He said in a puzzled voice. Brian arrived before the taxi my brother had called. We greeted each other and he was genuinely delighted to see me. He immediately called his wife and told her he was bringing a visitor home. My brother then called while I was still connected to the airport Wi-Fi and I told him that I was going to go with Brian and he would drive me to the hotel. Before I finished explaining, he shouted and said, "Tina, you can't just go with a random man you spoke to once to his house." My phone was on loudspeaker, so Brian responded and said, "Don't worry, she is safe with us. You can call in 30 minutes and speak to my wife. We all eased, and Brian drove us to his house. When we got there, his lovely wife, Patience, welcomed me with a hug that was as big as her smile.

She was so mellow and had a voice that sounded like calm waves. She made me feel safe. There was a warmness in her eyes that made me feel relaxed. I read her facial features for any signs of animosity; surely, there had to be some. Her husband had just brought a woman they didn't know into their home, but no, she was filled with genuine poise as she led me onto the dinner table that was already set. It was a momentous moment for me, what this wonderful couple symbolized. They loved the Lord so much that when Brian got lost, he immediately knew what the reason was. He knew that he was led to me, and his wife understood that there was a reason why her husband was sent to fetch me. She had started making a quick meal when she was told we were on the way, so she brought hot and hearty comfort food to the table. As we ate, my brother called, and I immediately put him on loudspeaker and handed Patience the phone. He thanked them for taking me to their house and asked them to drive me to the hotel he had booked. Patience, with her calmness, said, "No, we won't be taking Tina to the hotel; she can stay with us here while we sort her out. She would be lonely in a hotel room and with no one, but if she stays with us for 2 weeks or so, we will help her find an apartment and set her up." My brother must have said Oh wow, the same time as me. She refused to take any money from him, and she said, "No, you don't need to give us money for food or accommodation, Tina is my sister in Christ, and so what I eat, she will eat. Keep your money, then use it toward paying for her apartment." I was speechless. Their home was filled with love. Their housemate gave up her bed so that I would be comfortable. There were amazing people and each day I was with them, Brian helped me find my stride spiritually. All the questions I had were answered. We would go to church together and he and his pastor assisted me in harnessing my gift. We spent the better part of 14 days immersed in bible study. He taught me most of the things I know about God. I then stayed with Brian and Patience for 2 weeks as they helped me find my own place.

When I found the place, it was with a bubbly and loving woman whom I called Auntie Sue. We loved each other from the first time we met. In her home, I felt like I belonged. She treated me so well and no one would have ever guessed that I was just a tenant in her house. As our relationship grew stronger, we began talking about our families and where they come from and in those conversations, we found out that my grandmother and Aunt Sue's mother were first cousins that actually grew up together! Look at God. With the support of a woman who had become like a mother to me, I began to spread my wings to find my place in the promised land, to soar the skies like an eagle.

"Now to Him who is able to do, immeasurably more than all we ask or imagine, according to his power that is at work within us."

Ephesians 3:20

Why we Pray.

Wow! That is all I can say. I saw the Same God that the Israelites saw; I saw the God of Abraham, Isaac, and Jacob's work in my life. Miracles didn't just happen in the Bible; they happen right now too in our lives because He is the Same God. He is unchanging. He is called the Father of Lights who does not change like shifting shadows. (James 1:17) because He will never be less than He is now. The God that revealed himself in miraculous ways in the past is not different from the God that is here and moving things in our lives right now. How can we not call this an actual miracle? The Lord whispering the name of a person into my ear and then that person being led to help me is something that shows us that He is a miracle-working God who keeps showing up for His children. Just as He did for the Israelites, the Lord parted the "red sea" for me.

"Lord, when I get to Canada, may you make my path straight. May you align everything according to your will?" The spirit prayed for me and spoke. "In the same way, the Spirit helps us in our weakness. We do not know what we ought to pray for, but the Spirit himself intercedes on our behalf. 27: And he who searches our hearts knows the mind of the Spirit because the Spirit intercedes for God's people in accordance with the will of God." Romans 8:26-27

Remember that prayer I did in the park in Dubai? When I thought I was just mumbling and brushed it off? Well, it turns out that I was led to pray that way because when the Holy Spirit intercedes on our behalf, we say things that we ourselves may not have had the capacity to pray about. Prayer is how God lets us in on His will for us. He made it a point of contact between Him and Us so that He may be able to do what He wills to do in this physical, visible realm that we live in, from the invisible spiritual realm. Read that again.

I didn't know what I ought to pray for when I was praying in that park, but God knew it and the Holy Spirit led me to utter the prayer. This is because God knows what we need more than we do, He has seen our future and so He aligned my prayer to be in accordance with His perfect will for me. Prayer is the key to bringing down what God has already decreed for us; it pulls things the Lord already has laid down for us in His spiritual realm and brings them down to us in our physical realm. So, I had to unlock what the Lord had set for me by specifically praying for it the way I did, by letting the Holy Spirit guide me to utter the words I did. One might ask why God didn't just give it to me since He says in Isaiah, "Before you call on me, I will answer"? The reason is that Some things can only happen AFTER you pray for them; they will not happen if they are not prayed for;

that is why the Holy Spirit intervenes by guiding us on what to pray for or by interceding for us through wordless groans as the Book of Romans states. There are things in our lives that will not happen unless we pray for them and God with his grace, leads us on how to pray for these things if we walk with Him. Sam Storms elaborates on this and says, "We must never presume God will grant us apart from prayer what He has ordained to grant us only by means of prayer." God knows how our journey will end, as well as the means to get there and guides us on how to pray.

God's Manifest Presence

This is when God's presence is revealed to us in a way that is clearly tangible, convincing, and experiential. When it feels like a coincidence but is just too good to be just a mere one. When you cannot explain how everything seemed to have been connecting together for you, as if pieces of a puzzle are all being clearly laid out, and you experience God in ways you cannot begin to even fathom, that is the manifest presence of God. When I arrived in Canada, it dawned on me that the Lord had begun orchestrating this long ago and was now making everything align. When Brian somehow found himself lost on the road he drives every day, it is proof of how God will align everything in your favour. The sovereign hand of God aligned my footsteps and led me to the people that were to become my divine helpers. There is no way it was a coincidence that the same Brian I had somehow spoken to years ago about God was the same man that ended up picking me up from the airport, taking me to his house and continuing our spiritual conversations from where we left them many years ago. Brian was in the right place at the right time. It can only be the manifest presence of God. I experienced God in His glory. The Lord introduced me to Brian and then put him aside for when the time was right. From the time I had a Skype call with him to the time

Tina Butau

I came to meet him in person, a lot had changed in my life. I had now encountered God and could now relate to what Brian was telling me, as compared to the first time when I didn't even know much about how God works in our lives or how present He is. So, God was piecing this together all these years, and I didn't even have a clue that even in those times when I was struggling and being fired from my jobs, God was moving me from that place and directing me to where I was supposed to be. It dawned on me that when I prayed and cried that the Lord favours some and hates me, when I cried and said Lord, what have I done to deserve this punishment from you, the Lord was just working and moving things and people so that they would come to meet me at my time of need. The patience of God. Imagine if your child comes into your room and scolds you for not planning a party for his birthday. The child will call you all sorts of names, not knowing that you have already paid for a caterer, you have had the best baker to make them a themed cake, and you have been calling their friends and telling them it is a surprise. How would you feel? Just because this child didn't see you working on their birthday party doesn't mean you aren't planning the best party of their life. While I was asking God why things were happening, he was winning battles for me. Something was fighting my Canada trip and God came through and showed that where He has opened, no man can shut. Imagine, a stranger bought me a whole plane ticket for $2500, he happened to be with his phone the instant I needed him, and he also had that money kind of just waiting for me. It made me feel so guilty that I would pray and accuse God of doing nothing because I couldn't see anything, yet He was going all out, aligning everything to work out for my good.

There are also several places I could have ended up in while looking for accommodation, but God aligned everything so that I would live with someone who is related to me even when we didn't know. He knew I needed family in this faraway land, and He made sure I landed in the arms of one of the most loving and genuine people I know. He was setting all that up for me. What other love could come close? I experienced Him as Jehovah Jireh because He provided for me even things that I didn't even know I needed. All my encounters with God have made me look at everything differently. If something fails, instead of crying and asking why God took it away from me, I pray and say, "God, you know the reason why this didn't work because you are omnipresent and omnipotent. I don't know what you saw but I know that as long as I let You order my footsteps, You will never lead me into a ditch or trap." Instead of asking why, I say thank you because I know that his plans will never hurt me. So, knowing what I know now, that time I got fired twice in the same couple of months, I should have sat down and asked the Lord where he was trying to lead me instead of scolding Him and calling Him an unfair father. Not seeing Him at work doesn't mean He is not at work in our lives.

Part 2 of the book

In this part, I will not be narrating my past as I had been doing in part 1. Some of the things are now in the present or future. This is where I am going to take you to the deep end.

Chapter - 6

Mary Magdalene Season
of My Life

*"You are my hiding place; you will protect me from trouble and
surround me with songs of deliverance"*

Psalms 32:7

"I have done absolute fasts, I have cried to the Lord, I have done everything I could, so what do you mean when you say you are still getting attacks." My brother said in a weary voice. I was determined to end this but somehow it wasn't going away. You see, just like Mary Magdalene, I was plagued by demons. I was a veritable prisoner of demonic afflictions. I was a tormented soul who spent her days morose and devastated. I didn't know what the Lord wanted me to do. I had been prayed for, and I had spoken to some of the best pastors and intercessors. Mighty and anointed men of God had prayed for me.

My only sibling had gathered his church friends and prayer warriors to pray for me but none of that helped.

One day, when I had just had enough, I went to my knees and cried to the Lord. I asked, why won't you deliver me, aren't you the All-powerful God? So how come you are failing to deliver me, and I instantly got a response. The Holy Spirit showed me a vision. In that vision, I was on my knees praying and as I was praying, chains were being broken, things that looked like glass were being shuttered, and creatures were scritching away. There was a bright light that was shining around me and in that instant, I knew exactly what was required of me. I didn't need anyone else to pray for me; I needed to pray for myself. I was supposed to do what is called self-deliverance. I thought the Lord couldn't hear me, but I wasn't going to him; I was going to other people and asking them to pray for me; that's why nothing was happening. Not to say they weren't spiritually strong; no, it was because that was my journey. I had to self-deliver by praying to God for myself through my Lord and Saviour Jesus Christ. As my friend Emily and I were talking about these attacks, we got a revelation that I needed to openly rebuke and declare that I am a child of God and that my body belongs to Jesus. I needed to confess with my own mouth that my body is the temple of God and that the only spirit that was allowed to have anything to do with me was the Holy Spirit. The issue that was making it hard for the many prayer warriors to cast out these demons was that I hadn't denounced these attacks with my own mouth, so the demons still had a binding. The other issue that Emily and I reached at was that because I hadn't rebuked them out loud, they took advantage of that and still had a ground to stay.

We have authority over our bodies, and I needed to exercise it. So, the people who prayed and fasted for me were doing a wonderful job; I just needed to take charge and face these things head-on and admonish them in Jesus' name.

Only God could save me, just like Mary Magdalene who was plagued by seven demons; only Jesus could save her. No man or woman of God could do it except for the Lord Himself. Miraculously, I was saved from these attacks and just like Mary, my demonization only served to magnify the Goodness of God and the greatness of His grace. After deliverance, Mary followed Christ and for me, subsequently after my self-deliverance, my name was changed both physically and spiritually to Tina which means follower of Christ. Isn't God just wonderful? The Same God who delivered Mary and then followed her delivered me and gave me a name that means to follow him, and a person's name speaks to their purpose so essentially, I was Mary Magdalene in that season of my life because what happened to her, happened to me too. The beauty of all this is when the Lord heals you; He heals you completely. (PSALMS 41:3) Mary's and my emancipation from these demon afflictions was done to completion.

Having been freed from all this, I was tasked with yet something bigger than me. I wasn't sure I would be able to, but being a follower of Christ means I have to speak about Him and also do His work. The Lord tasked me with praying for the people who are bound by those spirits from the darkness. This can be sorcery or any form of evil spirits. For some, I am given the burden to call/visit and pray with them but for most, I pray for them on my own. As an intercessor. I was given the grace by the Holy Spirit to focus and intercede for others who may be under the affliction of evil spirits. I carry with me compassion and sensitivity to pray for the people around me.

I had to experience how demons afflict a person for me to be able to understand what spiritual warfare is. I had to learn it and then be able to deliver myself from it for me to be able to deliver someone else from it. I will take you back a little, I said, I went to people who were strong in spiritual warfare, so how did they gain that muscle? They had to go through it as I did, at least that is true for the ones I went back to ask.

There is very little information out there about the spiritual world and even though it was a painful experience, I thank God that he chose me to be amongst the people He has shown what we as Christians are up against. The Lord had chosen this path for me already, remember that man Brian, who told me about this years ago and I had stopped talking to him? I got reminded of this when he heard about someone I had prayed with, Brian said to me, remember the Holy Spirit told you that you would be doing exactly what you did for this woman, and you denied it? This is what happens with the things of God when He wants to use you, He will do it in a way that would make you understand why it had to be you.

I know that most people do not want to talk about demonic afflictions or attacks because there is a negative stigma around those issues. Even in churches, when a person is delivered from demons, that person will always be referred to, "That woman who had demons, have you forgotten about her?" It is easy to dismiss or not believe that there is spiritual warfare, but the bible clearly states that "we do not fight against flesh and blood but against the principalities, against power, against the rulers of the darkness of this age, against spiritual hosts of wickedness in the heavenly places." Ephesians 6:12

What do you think this scripture means? Take a moment and reflect on this word. What really does it mean?

What are Demons/Evil Spirits

Demons or evil spirits are spirits that are earthly bound and are spirits that do not have a body and crave greatly to be inside a body. They prefer human bodies and without a body, they cannot express their nature. An example is a demon of prostitution; it must have a body for it to be able to show itself through. They are tied up to the need of the human body for them to express themselves. They need a human body to satisfy their desires. So, each time a prostitute uses their body while under the influence of a demon, they make it stronger, and their craving becomes more and more. As with drugs or substance abuse demons. Another common one is the gambling demon; each time you 'use' it to make money, your need to keep making more from it arises. Watch on YouTube the video called "Self-Admitted Gambler Describes Turning "Demonic" As She Feeds Her Addiction." By Dr. Phil.

Each time you allow this spirit to work through you by exhibiting its desires through your body, the demon begins to evolve, thus becoming stronger and more powerful within you. That is when you find people throwing a fit when their addictions are not met.

A demon cannot possess the Christian body because it is already belonging to the Lord. The Bible says our bodies are the temples of God but what a demon can do; it can influence a person; it can afflict but not possess because to possess is to own and the Lord already owns us. What it does though, is to look for parts in you that aren't fully given to the Lord by that, I mean that which causes you to sin. So, for example, if your sin is in your tongue, the Lord is not in it because God cannot look at sin as it is said in Habakkuk 1:13 "Your eyes are too pure to look on evil" So those places in you that aren't for the Lord can be influenced by a demon. A demon can influence the areas of your life where the Holy Spirit and Christ's nature are not in effective control.

We are surrounded by evil spirits, and this is an unfortunate reality. We are not safe; our children are not safe. The devil comes to kill, steal, and destroy and sometimes targets our children. We must cover our children in prayer before they leave for school. We must teach them to pray and instil our Christian values in them.

In Zimbabwe, there was a time when boarding schools were getting constant reports of satanism and demon afflictions in schools; it is said that some of the children developed canine teeth and bloodshot eyes, while another pupil's skin reportedly took the colours of a snake, and other children were said to be mimicking animals. The education minister Lazarus Dokora was called to these schools, and he dismissed that it was evil spirits at work stating that, and I quote, "People might call it 'Satanism' because of what they hear at their churches" … "We receive such reports from time to time but without scientific proof, there is no way we can confirm satanism exists in schools. In actual fact, the kids suffer from anxiety." (Anadolu Agency, 2015) "Another case was reported in 2012 at Yemuranai Primary School in Mufakose Harare, where over 30 pupils became hysterical, among them, Grade One and Two children who became violent, exhibited extraordinary strength and spoke in unusual voices." (The Sunday Mail, 2017)

He is not the first person to dismiss evil spirits and how they roam the earth looking for prey. A lot of people will easily give a demonic plague a medical diagnosis. This is because it is easier to name it something you understand. Many people do not want to talk about it, but I believe that the Holy Spirit put this on my heart for me to raise spiritual awareness around this issue. Demon possession is an affliction, not a sin. These tormented people are not willful malefactors. The Bible speaks about how these evil spirits spoke through the lips of those whom they tormented (Mark 1:23-24, Luke 4:33-35) This could have been the case with those poor children I spoke about earlier. Afflicted people behave and react differently depending on the evil spirit plaguing them, but we cannot give it a name of a disease that exhibits similar symptoms just so that we can avoid the fact that evil spirits are at play. Scripture makes a very clear distinction between demon possession and diseases such as epilepsy and paralysis (Matthew 4:24).

How to Pray for Deliverance from Evil Spirits

So, I will start with my own experience of how I overcame it. It was Praying the word. The Same God that cast out demons from so many people that are said in scripture is the Same God that still brings deliverance to us today. By praying the word, we will be aligning ourselves under the authority of God, and we can only act in the authority of God when we are under His authority. We have to live by the word for us to be able to use it to pray effectively.

Praying the Word is to read relevant scriptures in a spirit of prayer and letting the meaning and context of that verse or chapter inspire your thoughts and you let it become your prayer. Personalize the scripture and where it allows, put your name in it.

The one scripture that I prayed and felt an instant result from was Psalms 51. It put into perspective everything I needed to know about praying the word. Praying through scripture is helpful because it ensures that our prayers are shaped by the will of God. It is also a way of reflecting God's power from heaven to earth. Jesus said, in His name, we will cast out demons, and when we pray the word, we are already praying in the name of Jesus so there is no chance that the evil spirits will dwell where the Holy Spirit dwells.

Chapter - 7

The Gideon Season of My Life

*"God says, I will pour out my Spirit on all people.
Your sons and daughters will prophesy, your young
men will see visions, your old men will dream
dreams."*

Acts 2:17

"Please take me back Lord, take me back," I shouted as I rolled hysterically on the floor, weeping. I mumbled inaudible things through my hands and choked on my sobs. Hot tears streamed down my cheeks as I tightly shut my eyelids hoping that if had squeezed them hard enough, I would somehow end up back into the vision that I had just come out of. It was the most beautiful place, and I didn't want to come back from it. I had seen and held children that were mine. They looked so delicate and perfect, and I wished I could bring them back with me to this physical realm. In my vision, I stared in amazement at the babies that were being called mine. I could see some resemblances. They were just beautiful. When I snapped out of the vision, all I wanted was to go back. I then prayed to the Lord, begging him to take me back but I soon realized that the things of God didn't work like that. Nothing one can do in their own strength and might can take you back to a vision. I had been given a snippet of my future and I wanted to see more of it; I wanted to go back and see how the story ended. In desperation to have a continued vision, I prayed again hoping that if I prayed hard enough, I would be given the vision again. When that didn't happen, I asked the Lord to confirm that this vision was from Him. I said, "Lord if this really was you, show me something physical that proves that this vision was really from you." This was my prayer. I earnestly recited Gideon's prayer and said, "If now I have found favour in your eyes, give me a sign that it is really you talking to me." Judges 6:17

I didn't think that the Lord would actually indulge me; I just prayed.

I felt a strong desire to keep praying, so I took my Bible once more. I went to 1 Samuel 2 and began reciting Hannah's prayer. After that, I went to sleep. I slept soundlessly the entire night, and a loud sound awoke me. It felt as though someone had banged or knocked at my patio glass door, so I woke up and went to see. When I got there, there was a bird laying the exact number of eggs as the number of children God had shown me in my vision. I quite simply fell on my knees and broke down. The walls around me were closing in, I couldn't breathe, and my heart was so full, I thought it would burst! So, the Lord had really answered my prayer? He had given me physical confirmation just as I had asked. I couldn't believe that the Same God that Gideon had called upon to confirm it was Him had shown Himself to me the same way He had done for Gideon. This reality gave me a panic attack. So, it really is the Same God. It dawned on me that God confirms. He is patient and kind, He could have said to Gideon and to me, "Forget it; I want people who have faith in me that won't challenge me to show them a sign." He didn't say that He came through and confirmed it.

When we are learning to hear God's voice, we need to ask God to confirm his word. And from my experience, God doesn't just start by throwing you into the deep end, He will begin to say small things to you for you to familiarize yourself with His voice. I have had encounters where the Holy Spirit whispered small things in my ear like, "Do you see that car in front of you? Slow down a bit because the driver in the red car is going to make a drastic lane change and as soon as I reduced my speed, surely, that driver did exactly what I was told he would do. So, God basically will start from the ground up. He will help you develop your spiritual muscle before He can give you the big things. At this time, it is wise to ask for confirmation because it will still be difficult to discern between God's voice and our thoughts or emotions. The emotional voice greatly mimics how the Lord speaks to us and so without having the proper discernment, we may easily conclude that it was God saying this while it could have just been our emotions.

Your Dreams are meant for you, only you.

God gave me a vision for my life because He wanted me to prepare. Just as He does with all of us. God prepares us by giving us visions and dreams of what the upcoming season of our lives will hold, but the devil also has the capability of posing himself as God. If we are not careful and pray for our visions, we risk being shown something that isn't of God, and we follow that misleading path. A vision or dream is something that is in the spiritual realm that hasn't yet been manifested into the physical realm; that is why when you have a dream or vision, you must pray to protect it as well as not tell it to other people. The devil is unable to see the plans that God has for us but is capable of interfering with them when they come to light.

This then gets us to the issue of spiritual warfare. We serve a good God that will come to our rescue when we call but that doesn't mean we need to relax knowing our Father is the Highest. As you grow stronger in your relationship with God, you aggravate the enemy and that means there will be no rest for you. It is your duty to pray and cover all that is dear to you. When we are given a dream, we should try as much as possible to be silent about it. Your vision wasn't intended for you to publish to everyone.

Even God urges us to do this as it is said in Proverbs 17:28 "Even fools are thought wise when they keep silent; with their mouths shut, they seem intelligent. Silence is a great virtue, and we should have the wisdom to know when to speak. Not everyone has good intentions for your life, if you naively think that everyone around you will be happy with your progress, you will be in great danger. There are people in life whose primary goal is to ensure that you are not successful, if you tell them your dream, they will crush it before its fulfilment. Try not to be like Joseph. The Lord gave him a dream and he ran to tell his brothers about it and then they plotted to kill him for his dreams. Genesis 37:9

"Joseph had the sort of pride common in the favoured and blessed. He was so focused on how great his dreams were for *him*, he didn't begin to consider how the dreams would sound in the ears of *others*." Enduring Words Bible Commentary.

Most people including me are guilty of this, thinking that our dream would excite the people around us so we blabber about the dream, naively thinking it would make the next person happy for us.

Tina Butau

Some people around you may appear to be innocent and harmless; they are like wolves in sheep's clothing; you will only know just how evil they are when they have succeeded in crushing you so be careful about whom you tell your dreams to. The Bible says in Jeremiah 17:9, "The human heart is the most deceitful of all things; and desperately wicked. Who really knows how bad it is"? There are some things that shouldn't be said, a vision or dream is something God intends for you and sometimes only you. The story of Saul sheds more light, (1 Samuel 10:14-16) God led Saul to the prophet Samuel when he lost the donkeys he was tending to. Saul was told by the prophet of the Lord that he would be king, but he kept it in his heart. He practised great wisdom and silence when he returned home to his uncle and told him that the prophet only shared the location of the donkeys, and he said that is all he was told. He didn't tell him the part of him becoming king. He didn't lie to his uncle, he simply shared only what was necessary. This too is what is required of us when we are given the privilege to see what our future holds. Unfortunately, most people learn about this a little too late. When our dreams are later interfered with, that is when we begin to regret and cry foul. Yes, some dreams will still come true even after they were tampered with, but that takes a lot of prayers and spiritual fighting. Yes, Joseph's dreams came true because God had intervened, but he could spare himself some of the hardships he endured because of his loudmouth. We too may end up taking the longer route to our destination because we had alerted the enemy of the road we were using and they went to set traps in our way; they set landmines and rerouting takes a lot of willpower and patience. If we hadn't told the enemy which route we would be taking, we would have gotten to our destination much faster and maybe more swiftly. We need to save ourselves from avoidable hostility by keeping quiet. Don't put yourself into bondage because of your words.

Yes, It is you He wants.

Then again still on Gideon because this is the season we are in, Gideon doubts his own ability to be used by God. Gideon thinks of himself as unworthy. He did not see himself the way God saw him and responded to God's call with fear and resistance. He went on telling God about how he was the least in his family as if God didn't already know that when He chose him to do the work. When the Lord shows us how bright our future is, we tend to ask ourselves if we are worthy or to look down upon ourselves. Like Gideon and I did. I have had a lot of visions where I came out saying, "Yeah Lord, that can't be me." I have said things with my own mouth that were against me. The moments when I thought something was too good to be mine, I rejected it by saying this can't be for me; this ratchet girl like me couldn't have or achieve this. I did this not knowing how powerful words were upon my life. Our words have the power to change a situation that was intended for good. A lady named Pastor Alec had prayed to God for children, but she failed to conceive for 5 years; she tried everything until one day, an intercessor prayed for her and told her that there was a word that she had come in agreement with, that cursed her womb, and she asked God to reveal what this was. She saw that when she was only 17 years old, her nieces and nephews would irritate her and make so much noise such that she said out loud that she never wanted to ever have children of her own. Those words bound her even years later when she tried to have children and failed. She then prayed, repented, and denounced her words and the Lord heard her, and she became pregnant that day. Our words have so much power that they can burden our spirit. "Our words have the power to destroy and the power to build up" Proverbs 12:6. Our words have the power to alter our dreams. You can be shown something today, and it will not manifest if you speak negatively about it. Our words to ourselves should be positive and affirming. Be kind to yourself with your words. You cannot expect other people to believe in you if you cannot believe in yourself.

Speak positively about everything that concerns you. Make affirmations about yourself. Each day, tell yourself that you are worthy, tell yourself that you are loved by God, tell yourself that you will go far, tell yourself that you are blessed. Do not continuously say a situation is hard; speak positively about it. Speak positively to your children. Your words make or break your children, so choose them wisely. Positive reinforcement is needed.

Chapter - 8

The Tabitha / Dorcas
Session of My Life

*"Father of the fatherless and protector of widows is
God in his holy habitation."*

Psalms 65:5

"I need it to be an orphan auntie. As I feel, this girl is an orphan, has passed her O Level with flying colours and has no money to proceed to A level," I said to my aunt Trish. I had been unable to sleep for days because I had something weighing heavy on my heart. I felt a longing, a hunger to find this girl, a girl that I didn't even know about. I didn't know where or how I would find her. Let me take you back to a few days before this call. I had a vision of an orphan child who needed to be taken to school. I didn't know where to find her but the more and more I dismissed this subject, the more it weighed heavily on me. I didn't know what I was meant to do but I knew that Auntie Trish could help me, so I called her. "The Lord has put this on my heart. I feel that I need to help a girl stranded in Zimbabwe. Can you call your contacts and ask if they have anyone that meets this criterion? She obliged. Auntie Trish was a strong, God-fearing woman I met in a group for single mothers and orphans years ago. She always used to say that the comments I made in the group were full of wisdom and love. She then fostered a relationship with me and loved me genuinely. Auntie Trish called her contacts, and she came back to me elated because she had found just the girl that matched the description. She was a very intelligent girl who had passed her O level with flying colours. She had 11 As but had no money to proceed. Her sister sold freezies on the roadside to provide for the girl. We will name her Yolanda. There were people who had asked organizations to help Yolanda get a scholarship but the only one that came through needed her to buy school supplies herself and she was unable to afford them, so the scholarship went up in flames. Yolanda spent the school year selling freezies on the roadside to try and raise money for uniforms for the next year but that was just going to be impossible because her freezies were being sold for 10 cents each. Auntie Trish gave me her sister's number and I called and said, "How are you guys, my name is Tina, and I was given your number by my auntie; she told me about Yolanda's situation, and I would like to assist her." "How did you know about Yolanda"? she asked. "To be honest with you, God sent me. I was given her profile days ago and I was tasked with finding her, so now that we are here, let me tell you what I will do for Yolanda. I will pay for her school fees, buy her uniforms, pay for extra lessons so that she catches up with everyone and buy her a laptop and textbooks," I said. I know that I must have sounded very stupid because we both gasped. For her sister, it may have been a delight but for me, it was shock. What had I just said to this person? Did I even know what I had committed myself to? You see, I had literally just arrived in Canada. I had no job. I couldn't even afford to send money to my daughter and here I was promising a now-celebrating family that I would rid them of their greatest burden. The conviction in my voice scared even me. When they were all crying on the phone and thanking me countless times, I heard myself say, "Don't thank me, thank God who did this. Also, Yolanda, you should keep praying because the God of orphans and widows is listening. Look, He has just sent me to you." I hung up and cried. I asked myself what I had just done.

It had only been a few hours since I had uttered things that I didn't know or understand, and I was nestled deep in my thought. The conversation had unfolded not as I had either intended or expected. The door was knocked loudly, and I dragged my feet to open it; I like to imagine that I looked like a sleepwalker coming out of a trance because as soon as I opened it, Aunt Sue said in shock, "Why do you look like that? What is stressing you? I didn't tell her what had happened, so I simply said I had a headache. I didn't lie; I did have a headache now from all the thinking. We sat in the lounge, and she told me out of the blue about a place where her daughter had worked that paid a little over minimum wage. As she spoke, I wrote the name of the company down and I casually applied for a call centre job.

The following day I received a call to come for an interview and I then got the job instantly. I was in awe. I couldn't believe how it happened so fast.

So, the Lord knew that I would get this job. The Holy Spirit led me to tell this family that I would help them when I didn't even know what I would eat the next week, let alone send anyone money. I experienced God as "Father of the fatherless, …in God's Holy habitation." Psalms 68:5

This takes us to this wonderful season in my life when I walked into my calling. I will share with you my experience with knowing your calling and harnessing it. If God calls you, He gives you the means.

Being Led into Your Calling.

Matthew 13: 31-33 "[31]He told them another parable: "The kingdom of heaven is like a mustard seed, which a man took and planted in his field. [32] Though it is the smallest of all seeds, yet when it grows, it is the largest of garden plants and becomes a tree, so that the birds come and perch in its branches." [33]He told them still another parable: "The kingdom of heaven is like yeast that a woman took and mixed into about sixty pounds [b]of flour until it worked all through the dough."

These parables show us that the things of God start from a small thing that then grows into something big. His calling for you may begin as a small voice or a word. God speaks to our hearts regarding why He called us, and we grow into our callings. As I had been given a small part of my calling, the bigger picture came. I began to understand what God had called me to do. I knew that I was going to be helping orphans and single mothers. As we are led into our callings, we need to listen to even the smallest of instructions because God uses that to unlock whatever is supposed to come next. Just as those parables stated, growth or rising doesn't start from something big; it begins with a little thing that grows into something big.

If we look at Jesus, He also needed to grow into His calling. Jesus could have been dropped from heaven in a gold chariot as an adult man ready to change the world, but God made sure that he started as a baby. He too had to grow, as the bible says in Luke 2:52

52 And Jesus grew in wisdom and stature and in favour with God and man.

As Jesus grew in these aspects, it meant that He also grew in his usability by God. Just like Jesus, we too need to grow in the Lord so that we can grow into our callings. That we may be led into our callings.

Walking in a manner worthy of your calling (Ephesians 4:1)

What really is a calling? I learnt from Pastor Tony Evans that "Calling can be defined as the customized purpose God has ordained for you and you alone to accomplish in order to bring Him the greatest glory and the maximum expansion of His Kingdom." Your calling is a created purpose, the reason why you were created/made. A year or so ago, my friend had a fridge that stopped working; the deep freezer wouldn't freeze. She was frustrated because the freezer wasn't doing what she had bought it to do.

Have you ever wondered why your life seems stagnant? Could it be because you aren't fulfilling your purpose and the Lord is trying to get you to grow? We often ask God why He isn't moving things in our lives, but are we allowing God to grow us so that He can enable us to fulfil our purpose? God didn't create you because He had run out of other things to do or for fun. He created you to fulfill your purpose. God says, "I knew you before you were created in your mother's womb," meaning to say when He created you and allocated you a parent, He already knew what you would need to do once you got to this land. There is something that we grew up being told that when a person is born, they come out with their fists clenched because they are carrying their gifts and purpose in their hands. Now that I know what I know, I'm asking myself if this wasn't true? You cannot tell yourself your calling because you don't know it; it's similar to asking the bed you sleep in, "Bed, why were you made? The bed has no idea but the person who created the bed will have your answers. I bet if you could find that creator, he would say something like, "I created this bed so that after a long day, a person can dive into it and relax. And rest. It is comfortable and it is the most important piece of furniture" The bed didn't know this about itself because it didn't create itself. Have you asked your creator why you were made? If you do not pursue your calling, you will spend the rest of your life wishing you were somebody else. There is a misconception that a calling from God means being in ministry alone. This isn't true. A calling isn't only about being called to do ministry; we are called to the Kingdom. Not everyone can be a pastor; someone must be a doctor, and another must teach. Ultimately serving God can be your calling and we serve God in different ways. Your calling is something that you do anyway without getting gratification for it.

Dorcas knew what her calling was. She didn't let societal limitations hinder her from following her calling. I called this the Dorcas season of my life because, like her, I was called to help orphans and single mothers. I have changed the lives of many single mothers and orphans literally. Looking back, I realize that the Lord put those people in my life because only I could take them from where they were to bring them to where they should be.

The same God that enabled Dorcas to continue in her calling is the Same God that was present when I was growing in mine and is still with me. Like Dorcas, I changed the lives of single mums and orphans while I was single; I suppose it wasn't easy for her but somehow God gave her the strength to carry on. I can definitely tell you that it wasn't easy for me. There were times that I cried out and told the Lord that I would never help anyone again because the people I had helped were those who turned around and destroyed things that I had taken years to build. That, however, didn't deter me because I knew that my gratification came from doing right by God, so I would get up and start to rebuild again. It is said in the bible in Acts that Dorcas got ill and died. It doesn't say what she got ill from. Let's imagine Dorcas was poisoned by someone she had once helped. Imagine the regret she felt or what she was going through in her last moments. But God being a wonder-working God, raised her from the dead. This means God let whatever afflicted Dorcas kill her so that he would raise her stronger and better. This is what I imagined happened to me when I was put in the shadows of death by people that I had once helped, loved, and regarded as family. You'd suspect that I then grew bitter and pledged to never help anyone in my life again. Well, you are wrong. I picked myself up and continued to walk into my calling. Why is that? It's because I know that I was called to be a bridge for God's people. This is my calling. I had to sit back and introspect. The thing I was doing wrong was to love people who were simply meant to pass through me and not stay with me.

For a moment I forgot that I needed to separate the things that bring me personal gratification from the things aligned with my calling. The first thing I had to do was to understand what it is I was really called to do. I was meant to be a bridge. A bridge is a structure or roadway that is designed to allow people to cross from one end to the other. So, what happens if the bridge is blocked? Others are unable to pass. That was my answer. Simple. So, I had to put measures in place to make sure that the bridge is never blocked, but I had to figure out why I ended up being in this predicament. I had to understand why people were quite literary trying to destroy me when all I had for them was love. I had to look within myself. I had attachment issues that were not resolved. My issues were getting in the way of God's greater plan because I didn't address them. I essentially broke my own heart by trying to make people who were passing through stay with me, forgetting that I am just a bridge. What are the things that you need to address before you step into your calling? If you do not do the necessary adjustments to your life and have an uncomfortable conversation with yourself, then you will hate your calling because it will always be entangled by the things that are personal. Moses had anger issues that caused him to disobey God; he must have addressed them first before walking into his calling. All that time serving God only for him to be hindered by his unresolved personal issues. His anger issues got in the way of him and God and as a result, he ended up not getting into the promised land. All those years he spent helping the Israelites and still not being able to get to the finish line because he didn't address his issues. Moses should have gone back to the Lord and said, "Father, your people are ungrateful, and I cannot deal with them." May you please intervene instead of taking it upon himself to do God's job. His assignment was to take God's children from one place into another, but it was never to discipline them because some things are only meant to be handled by God Himself. All these things are brought to light when you ask God to grow you for you to fulfill your calling. As you grow in Him, His glory shines brighter, and the light of the Holy Spirit shines in your life. This light will help you see where you are getting it wrong, the same way I saw where I got it wrong. You must let the Holy Spirit in you reveal the things within you that will hinder you from fulfilling your calling successfully.

How to be rooted in your calling

You can only be strongly established in your calling when you have experienced the presence of God. This is when you see His glory when you are doing things aligned with your calling. When your fulfilment comes from knowing that what you have done, you did for the Lord's glory to be seen and that what you did was good in the Lord's eyes, then you can be strongly rooted in your calling. You will be in a position to withstand any trials that may come your way. When the inevitable hard times come, when people begin to speak evil of you, when they begin to question your motive or if things go wrong then you will overcome all those. If you are not convinced of the call of God for your life, you will be easily uprooted. This is why you must know God's presence before you can operate in His power.

When you operate in God's power, He will "resurrect you when you are killed" (obviously not literally) while doing His work through your calling. You need not be afraid because He knew we would get into troubles like these when He gave us a prayer to use when we have no words of our own. Yes, when the pain really hits you hard, the praying words are erased from your tongue and because God knows everything, He gave us Psalms 35 for times like these. It says:

> "1 Plead [1]my cause, O Lord, with those who
> strive with me;
>
> Fight against those who fight against me.
>
> 2 Take hold of shield
> and [2]buckler,
> And stand up for my help.
>
> 3 Also draw out the spear,
> And stop those who pursue me.
> Say to my soul,
> "I am your salvation."
>
> 4 [a]Let those be put to shame and brought to
> dishonour Who seek after my life;
> Let those be [b]turned back and brought to
> confusion Who plot my hurt.
>
> 13 But as for me, [i]when they
> were sick, My clothing
> was sackcloth;
> I humbled myself with fasting;
> And my prayer would return to my own [5]heart.
>
> 14 I paced about as though he were my friend or brother;

I bowed down [6]heavily, as one who mourns for his mother.

15 But in my [7]adversity
they rejoiced And
gathered together;
Attackers gathered
against me, And I did
not know it;
They tore at me and did not cease;

Answering God's Call

The beauty of remaining in God as you do what He called you to do is that when things go wrong, He will be there to correct them. "Call on me and I will answer," is what the Lord said. Sometimes walking in your calling gets overwhelming but take heart and go on. Do not let your experience with the previous assignment stop you from starting the new one at your feet. Jesus served the Lord and he too got overwhelmed at times. Remember when He took Peter and his brothers and went away from everyone (Matthew 17:1) We too can take a break and start again. Some people are ungrateful, but their ungratefulness is not toward you but toward the one who sent you so when you get fed up, go to their creator, and lay your heavy burden on him. Vengeance is for Him; you just continue doing what you were called to do. Remember how ungrateful the Israelites were? They pushed Moses to the edge, and he was unable to get into the promised land because of what the ungratefulness of God's people led him to do. Do not be like Moses, when it gets tough, speak to the one who gave you your assignment so that He may deal with his people. Your calling could be in the medical field to help God's people as a doctor; maintain your grace because if you do not, you will end up killing the person you were meant to help. Your calling may be teaching; do it patiently because the child that you rudely dismissed because he was slow may be dealing with difficult parents and the Lord put you in his path so that he can get the grooming from you. If you were called to be a midwife and you treat those birthing mothers horribly, you risk killing a child that may have been a great preacher who will one day bring people to God.

Motherhood as a calling

I feel that this deserves its own topic because I think it is one of the greatest calls of all. You may have been called to be a mother, yes, a mother. Are you failing to conceive? Have you tried everything humanly possible to get pregnant and it just seems to not happen? Then maybe your calling is to become a mother to the motherless. People often look at barrenness as a curse, but it may actually be your calling. Let me explain. There are children born every day that are abandoned; they deserve a chance to live as much as other children, if someone is not assigned to be a mother to those children, then they will remain orphans. The Bible says God loves orphans, they are regarded as God's children and he pledged that "He would not leave them as orphans, He will go to them." (John 14:18) So maybe the fact that you are unable to carry any children of your own, the Lord is telling you to be a mother to His children and isn't that just a blessing? How are you different from Mary? God chose her to be the mother of His son Jesus Christ, and maybe He has chosen you to be the mother of His other children. You are the chosen ones, chosen to be Mothers to God's children. So yes, your calling could be exactly that, motherhood. If you feel this is you, I urge you to seek God regarding that matter. Pray and ask if he did not give you any biological children because maybe he had something more special in store for you, adoption. This was put on my heart and as I write it, I know it is directed at someone who has been questioning why God isn't answering their prayer, yet He promised. There is an encouraging story on YouTube called: Chloe-A story of infertility, Adoption, and God's love. It speaks about how God put a child in this couple's hearts. They thought they would have their own biological child but instead, everything was pointing them toward adopting this same baby that the Lord had made them love years ago. The Lord writes all our stories, He did say in Psalms 32:8 That "He will instruct you and teach you in the way you should go: He will counsel you with His eye upon you" So search deep within you and open up your mind to what the Lord may be trying to instruct you to do. I feel that the difference in callings is not spoken about as much as it should, so people may not regard parenthood as a calling. Mary and Joseph were called to be Jesus' parents and it is one of the greatest calls ever recorded in the history of men. What if this is your calling too? Your adopted child may not be the Messiah, but they may change their world in his own right. If the Lord set up parents for this baby before it came into this world, He knows the plans that He has for your child. Think deeply about this; it could be ministering to you and if it is, may the Lord give you that child that you so desire. Sometimes adoption then paves the way for your own children but maybe God would have wanted you to adopt your first child before having your own because when you have your own, the desire to adopt another doesn't burn as much as it does when you are longing, praying, and yearning for one.

We are all called differently, and it is our duty to seek God and ask Him what He called us to do. When you know what your calling is, do it graciously. Do it with love and even though it sometimes hurts, trust in the Lord that He knew you enough to assign this call to you. He knows your capabilities and sometimes the hardships are just meant to sharpen and refine us. They are meant to toughen us up as we grow. They boost our strength.

Chapter - 9

The Abraham Season of My Life

Pruned by God

I have been forced to walk away from a lot of people that were dear to me without completely understanding why I was made to just forget everything and move on. In most cases, my motive was totally misconstrued, or I was simply not given a chance to explain my behaviour or actions. I used to stress, thinking about all the things I wanted to say but the door seemed to have just been tightly shut. I questioned why God would make me walk away without giving me the opportunity to express myself. You see, I am a very expressive person; I knew that if I had just been given a chance to pour my heart out and apologize, I would have done so successfully, and I would have made the other person somehow understand why I did what I did. It was after looking at the way these doors were closed that I realized that God intended for them to remain shut and if I had been given even a moment's chance, I would have tried to open them. You see, for God to be able to use you effectively, He must first separate you from everything you know. Just as He did with Abraham, Genesis 12 vs 1: Go forth out of thy country, and from thy kindred" (KJV). He will separate you from friends, family, and people you love because He knows that their influence in your life will interfere with the journey that God Himself has set you on. And this works both ways. It is called God's pruning process. "Pruning is not a punishment for a Christian; it is a reward. God is the vinedresser who prunes the life of everyone who abides in Christ and bears the fruit of Christ. Spiritual pruning enhances spiritual growth by removing whatever inhibits spiritual growth" (Union University)

As I had learnt to hear God's voice more, I was made to believe that I was delusional because the people around me knew who I was before being called to follow Christ. Everything I was told, I used to share with them because I wanted validation, acknowledgement, or encouragement from them. None of what I said to them made sense, they may not have been so brutal to tell me to my face that I was crazy, but it sure was clear.

I was so desperate to be understood by people, without knowing that my relationship with God was very personal. It was supposed to be between me and Him and I was using my energy to make the people around me believe me about what God had said or was saying in my life. Their response to what I had told them about what God said to me affected how I heard God's voice so in order for The Lord to shut out every other voice, and leave only His, He had to prune me. "Pruning is when you selectively remove branches from a tree. The goal is to remove unwanted branches, improve the tree's structure and direct new, healthy growth." Davey Tree Expert 2018.

This is what God takes us through before he can use us. He prunes us and removes all the branches holding on to us to ensure that He is left with only you so that the energy you have is not wasted on the other branches but is utilized by you, the main brunch. Yes, it is a very painful process because a branch is something attached to the tree; cutting it off is like removing a part of it and yes, the tree will bleed, and you too will bleed.

So, I am going to use my experience with this to talk to you about broken relationships with friends and other "important" people in our lives. We first need to understand that God sometimes removes people from our lives because they have no place in where we are going next. Look at your life as though you were a train in a long transit. You are going somewhere but they are numerous stops within the journey. In those stops, you pick up some and drop off others. Some may have been on the train since the day it began the journey (your birth) and they will probably ride with you until you get to where you are going (family), but those that you pick along the way (friends/partners) may at one point exit the train the same way they were picked up unless they are still going the same direction that you are, then they may remain on the train. If along the way, one decides that they want to go on a different route, no matter how long or how far they have travelled with you, they must exit this train. When they do, the seat they occupy becomes empty, and you as the train moves, may feel their absence but that doesn't mean that if you stop for them, they will come back on. So, you must keep going because as you journey on, you might pick up someone along the way that will fill in that seat and if not, as the train goes on, you will get accustomed to having that particular seat empty and its lack of occupation will not affect you any longer. If this person is going where you are, they will always be on your train. The train cannot make a U-turn; it must keep going. So, whoever was dropped off at the last stop must either hop onto the next train that goes where they are going or count their losses as they stand at the station and watch you travel on. When you try to reverse an entire train to go back and pick up one person that left the train, there are a lot of risks and malfunctions that you are now subjecting the train to, so the best course is to keep going and become content with the memories as the only thing you are left with.

It isn't always that God will remove people from you or you from people because the people are bad. Sometimes God will be trying to call you to follow the path of your calling. And usually, you grow into your calling; it is something that you come to understand as you walk with God. So, growing into it means that they are habits and mannerisms that you will have to master and you can only master them yourself, and it is difficult to concentrate where there is a lot going on, so God will isolate you. This isolation often feels like a prison or dark cave if you do not fully understand why God has isolated you. Look at yourself as a fetus in a womb. It is dark and isolated; the only person you can make contact with is the person that you are in. You cannot talk to anyone about your growth; you cannot update them that now you are at this stage in your development. You will be in there for a very long time but as you are there, you will be growing and maturing. Just because the outside world cannot see you grow all the different parts of your developing body doesn't mean the person you are in doesn't see and feel the changes. It is often complicated if you get out of the womb before the time is up so for you to be fully developed, wait until the time to be released into the world comes.

When we are in this isolation, you are really not alone because someone is carrying you. God is carrying you. You do not have to worry about anything because you are covered and protected inside. You don't have to do anything at this point except to focus on your growth. If we could see that God is with us in every season, we would stop worrying. Listen to the song by Rebecca Dawn called Oh My Soul. It gets us to look back and see if God has ever failed us. It speaks about the faithfulness of God. Even when it feels as if He is not present, He is there. If we do not listen to God when He is telling us to isolate ourselves and hear only His voice, we risk listening to other voices that surround us that are not the voices of God. You may be living with other people whom you regard very highly, and their opinions seem to be valid regarding what God has said about your life. Do not listen to anyone who questions or ridicules what God has said about you; remember that it was told to you and you alone, so stick only to what God says and not to what others tell you about God. If He has said something in the past and it came to pass, what makes you think this too won't happen? Just because this message/ promise didn't come in a manner that you or people around you are familiar with doesn't mean God didn't say it or He won't do it. A good analogy of this is Abraham's story.

If Abraham had not listened to the people around Him, he would have most likely walked into God's will. Let me explain; Abraham had been talking to God and he would do everything the Lord guided him to do. His problems began when he wanted his wife to understand him, to validate his vision and encourage him. When he told Sarah that the Lord had told him that he would have a child with her, Abraham believed God's word and was prepared to wait or do whatever it took but Sarah changed his mind. He listened to what his wife said over what God had said. He gave someone the power to cross-reference his promise, his... Sarah thought she knew how God operated because she had never heard of anything quite like Abraham's promise so she translated his promise into something she could understand. She may have said, "Oh Abraham my love, I don't dispute that the Lord speaks to you, and I also don't negate that He did say you were going to have a child; all I'm saying is you really could have misinterpreted this vision. You heard correctly, but your interpretation must be wrong. I think that maybe God meant you should have the child with someone else." Thereby offering Hagar. This must have been an Ah huh moment for Abraham, his wife was saying very sensible things. She made sense, he had misinterpreted God. So, Abraham was led to make a grave mistake that would make generations suffer the consequences. One may ask why God agreed for Hagar to become pregnant when it wasn't his plan. This is the beauty of God, he can only tell you His will, but He does not force it on anyone. So, if He tells us something and we choose to believe the people around us, he lets us do our will because we all have free will. Abraham wasn't punished for his disobedience; he was simply left to suffer the consequences of his actions. Surely God could have sealed Hagar's womb, but he could not because that would mean He would have interfered with Abraham's will. He let him be. What Abraham did was delay his blessing because he decided to listen to what someone else told him about God. God doesn't need an interpreter or translator; His word is true. No matter how much it didn't make sense to Abraham, he should have known better. He should have been the wiser, judging from how far He and God had come. God's things are usually very hard to believe; of all the miracles, they are hard to comprehend; that is why heathens call the bible a fiction novel. If it is simple and straightforward, then how is it a miracle? If you can look at the situation with your own eyes and come up with a solution, then how then can we call it a miracle? God knew what He was saying to Abraham. It sounded ridiculous and impossible yes, but how then do we call God the God of the impossible if we cannot see him turn water into wine? If we cannot see Him make a virgin pregnant if we cannot see Him making a 90-year-old Sarah pregnant? His glory is seen through Him doing what men call impossible. His mightiness is shown when He parts the red sea. His power is shown when he confuses the tongues of those men on the tower of Babel. That is when we see God. He didn't put perfect stories in the bible because He wanted us to know that the bible giants like Abraham were flawed just like us. They made mistakes as we do but the Bible works as our guide. We cannot do as Abraham did because we saw how he suffered the consequences of his actions. We should learn from him and do what he should have done and not what he did. He listened to someone else who seemed to be making sense more than God. Is this you? Are you Abraham listening to Sarah? But have you forgotten where God took you from? If He was with you at that time when He said to leave everything you know and go there, what makes you think that He will abandon you now? " how long will you keep treating God with contempt, how long will you keep refusing to believe in him in spite of all the signs, he has performed amongst you" Numbers 14, 11. What makes you think that now you are misinterpreting the voice of God simply because what He is telling you is not aligning with what you think it should be? If He says the impossible, rejoice because you know you are a miracle in the making. Worry if He tells you that He is going to do something that you can already do for yourself by yourself. Start questioning where a vision/ dream came from if it is as easy as ABC because God works in ways we cannot see. He said in Isaiah 55 vs 8: Your ways are not my ways, and my thoughts are not your thoughts. He also says Trust in the Lord with all your heart and lean not on your own understanding. (Proverbs 3:)

So, trusting Him means knowing that even if you cannot see the light, you know that if God led you on this dark path the light is there somewhere. Even if you cannot see it, trusting Him means you know that somewhere in the midst of this confusion, He will make a way for you. I once went onto a slide called the leap of faith. It was a steep slide that didn't show where it would end. The vertical drop made sure that you wouldn't see where you would land. The 60-foot slide pushes you with tremendous speed through a tunnel infested with sharks and all you have to do is have faith that you will land somewhere safe. Hence the name, leap of faith. So, going onto this slide means that I had to trust the engineer who created this. I couldn't see where I'd land, I couldn't see if the sharks were close by, I couldn't hear anything except my scream but somehow, I had trust that I would land safely. Who did I trust? It certainly wasn't me because I didn't know what I was getting myself into, but I had faith that if others had been on the same slide and survived, I too surely will survive. That terrifying slide made me see God in a different light. If I could trust a human like me with my life even though I was terrified and had no idea where id land, surely, I could trust the God of the universe with whatever He has led me to no matter where I will land. If you have been on a plane, you have trusted the pilot; how do you know he is not an alien that would fly all of you into space? How do you know he won't fly you through the Bermuda Triangle? You don't know that he won't, but you have faith in him. You sleep on the flight and relax even though you have no idea what part of the world you are flying through because you know you are in safe hands. Can we offer the same amount of faith and trust to God? He will see us through. Even though we cannot see where we are right now, let us trust the pilot of our lives, He knows exactly where He is taking us. There will be turbulence on the way, heavy storms may come, and the winds may blow but He will see us through. Trust Him with all your heart, even when you don't understand what is going through.

I called this the Abraham Chapter because I learnt my lesson from Abraham. I listened only to God at this point in my life. People told me things that made sense; others told me that God didn't work that way, and a few more said I had misinterpreted God, but I held on tight. I knew that right at this moment when nothing made sense, He was there. I waited for my miracle Isaac; I did not listen to people and ended up having Ishmael who wasn't the promise. You too listen to God. What He has said will happen. It may not make sense to the people around you, but the promise is not for them; it is for you.

Habakkuk 2:3-4 For the vision is yet for an appointed time; But at the end, it will speak, and it will not lie. Though it tarries, wait for it; Because it will surely come, It will not tarry. "Behold the proud, His soul is not upright in him, But the just shall live by his faith."

Chapter - 10

The Hagar Season of My Life

"…and I will bless you; I will make your name great, and you will be a blessing."

Genesis 12:2

The Blessing of my life

"What did I do to deserve you?" I said as a gleaming light touched my eye. That light was hope. It was what I needed at this dark time of my life and this child that I didn't even know I needed wiped that single tear before it escaped my eyelid. I looked at her and then looked up to the sky as if I were expecting to see God smiling at me. I suppose He did because my baby had said something that only the Holy Spirit could have put on her heart. I was in the most difficult phase of my life when I was battling depression. I felt as though I was in the wilderness alone with my child as Hagar had been with Ishmael. I was feeling downcast and devastated and I was going back and forth trying to see if the Lord loved me at all. Stupid question I know, judging by where the Lord had taken me from, I clearly am forgetful just like the Israelites. I was questioning Him in prayer and asking if He cared. I used to sing a song that asked if God was with me as He once was. I was desperate for a word from Him but there was silence. I asked myself what I had done for Him to turn away from me. I was saying all these things in a loud prayer and once I was done, Chicco walked in, sat, and laid my head on her chest and said, "Mum, I wasn't prying but I heard your very bitter prayer and I felt that we needed to talk about it." That caught my attention and I looked at her. She continued to speak. This child reminded me of everything that the Lord had done, all the time that He never failed me. She began reminding me of my dreams and visions as well as the promises from God. She went on and said, "God is not a man that He should lie, you taught me that scripture in the book of Numbers, and mum, just because something isn't happening in the time that you want it to doesn't mean God lied. Do you not remember that you taught me that things happen in the spirit first and then they manifest in the physical at a different time?" I felt naked. I was called out by a child. But then again, was that being called out or being reminded? I needed to accept that I was wrong and that maybe I stopped hearing the voice of God because I was giving Him ultimatums and timelines when all He wanted from me was patience. I needed to sincerely acknowledge that God was at work even in those times when I couldn't see it. I had forgotten that the Lord says in Isaiah 46:11 "I have spoken it and I will bring it to pass; I have purposed it, I will do it. Chicco then said she would pray for me because I had clearly lost it. I thought to myself, Wow! In that moment, I just wanted to give birth to this girl again and throw myself a baby shower because wow. After that, I sat and began to introspect, a few minutes later she texted me to come upstairs. I went there and she ran me a bubble bath with rose petals and candles; her iPad was playing my favourite movie and there was a wine glass with orange juice on a tray. It was the sweetest thing ever. I took that bath with a smile and a warm heart. After that I thanked her and she said, "Mum, I know you aren't in the right state to continue our all-night prayers so will stay up all night by myself and finish them alone." We had given ourselves 6 days to pray the entire night then wrap up the last prayer when the sun came out. She asked me to go to sleep and said, "I will carry both of us in prayer; tonight, rest Mama." I couldn't believe my ears. It was as though I was being taken care of by my mother. I felt seen and loved in ways that I could not comprehend. The following day she said, "We have three more days of all-night prayer; Mama I know that you are going through a lot and you will not be able to continue. That doesn't mean that the prayers aren't going to go on. I will be doing them alone. Around midnight, she urged me to sleep; when I was in bed, she tucked me in and slid into the bed to massage me and scratch my back, all this while playing something called "Sleep with God's word by Soak in God's promises by the ocean." It is a soothing sound of ocean waves and a calm voice speaking the word of God in a serenading way. I didn't even know such a thing existed on YouTube. My baby would continue to massage and scratch until I drifted into sleep; she would complete this with a kiss on my forehead and then go back downstairs into the living room to do her all-night prayers. Around 6 as the sun rose, she would kneel and pray. She says having the sun come out as she prayed signified a new beginning. It reminded her of the scripture that says, "Joy comes in the morning."

For 3 days, my baby did this and completed her all-night prayers alone. I was astonished. So, this perfect human being was actually my child? As in mine? The Lord entrusted me with such a soul? I don't know what I did to deserve her. She is beautiful inside as she is on the outside. In her, all I see is God's glory. Momentarily, our prayers were answered. The very thing we had spent 6 days praying for had come to fruition. We saw the goodness of God and were so overjoyed. If He says a word, He will see it to completion. He is God that never falters. He comes through even when we thought he had let us down, He is gracious and faithful enough to keep his promises.

My Blessing!

Tina Butau

The Depths of Depression

A few months later My depression in this season had struck hard. I had sunken into its depths, and it was about to consume me whole. Remember, we are in the Hagar season, so like Hagar, there was a time when I was so desponded and cast down that I contemplated suicide. My suicidal thoughts were heavy because I wondered what would have become of my child if I died. Like Hagar, I was overtaken by thoughts of hopelessness. I know that somehow my daughter knew that I had sunk in this deep; she knew because she was the only person who knew my heart from the inside. When she was inside my body, there was a fire that burnt violently and she alone felt and saw it now that the fire was growing weak and going out, so she alone could rekindle its flame and she did it the best way she knew how, on her knees. She had seen my secret struggles and heard my silent tears, and she knew she needed strength to carry both of us through. I did have other people around me that were very close, but they didn't see or sense my depression, only my daughter did. So, she lifted her eyes to the mountains where her help comes from (Psalms 121: 1-3) and she stood on the Rock (Psalms 62:6) and it became both our refuge. She knew that her strength to deal with this by herself without her needing to reach out to any of the people in our lives came from the Lord. Her heart trusted in Him, and she was helped; Therefore, her heart greatly rejoices, and she sang songs to give Him praise when I was well again. (Psalms 28:7)

It dawned on me that I had succeeded in raising my baby to become a God-fearing teenager. I had done a good job of teaching her that God was the head of us. I was reaping those fruits of my labour as I experienced His greatness abundantly through my child. By God's grace, she was mature enough to understand that depression is real. Depression gets the most of us and if we do not turn to God, it will consume us. Suicidal thoughts have become rampant in recent years. There is no "typical suicidal person" and I know I am not the only one who has had those wicked thoughts. There are different factors that lead to suicidal thoughts but in my case, it was 2 things, depression and a history of a family member who had committed suicide. It is believed that when a family member commits suicide, that suicidal spirit will linger for generations to follow, so it is important to pray and denounce such spirits as well as receive therapy.

It is not that a person has these thoughts simply because they are weak or a coward as people say, at least that wasn't the case for me. I am strong; I have come so far to get here. I had everything I wanted; I was in a wonderful relationship where I was loved immensely, with someone that loved my child as if she was his. I had most of the things that I had ever wanted right in front of me. I was doing better than I could imagine but I was still depressed and just wanted to not exist. I would wear a smile and maintain my high-spirited behaviour around people but inside me was a tiny girl weeping, and that girl would take over me when I was alone. She would resurface because I tried to shut her out by wearing a smile and when that smile faded, she would be there waiting to be rescued. I was having PTSD from things that happened in my past and things that I went through when I was much younger. I pitied myself for growing up the way I did. I questioned a lot of things from my past and bitterness from back then was weighing me down. I was suffering from daddy issues that hadn't been addressed. I had been forced to become an adult because I had a child when I was still a child myself. I never got to fully recover from all that, and it was catching up with me. In short, I had so many things weighing me down and I was quite simply drowning. For some people, it is because they are in such a difficult situation or in great pain and they feel death is the only way out. Statistics show that "Suicide attempts happen 10 times more often than suicide deaths in women" (Chaudron & Caine, 2004) In Alberta Canada, "Women accounted for 58% of 1833 hospital admissions and 61% of 5,053 visits for attempted suicide."

If you, my darling is feeling depressed. Talk to someone about what's troubling you. The first thing to do is confront the issue that is making you desolate. My issue was really the childhood trauma I endured that I had never spoken about. I have someone in my life that I knew was there when I was younger, and I knew she loved me like her own child since I was a baby, so I turned to her. She is my mother's younger sister and I call her Mai MaTshu. Story is for another day. I called her and told her that I wanted to talk about my childhood. The first thing she addressed was that my father loved me, and he worshipped the ground I walked on. I thought it wasn't true because if that were the case, why then would he just up and leave with no explanation? Why did he break my heart? She said, "I know beyond doubt that your father loved you. Why he did what he did can only be answered by him, so I suggest that you pick up the phone and confront him." And so, I did.

"Ring ring, ring ring." The phone rang with the same urgency as my heartbeat. I was sweating and I didn't know what to say. As I was still trying to memorize my first sentence, I heard his voice saying, "Tina, hello, are you there?" I thought to myself, okay, we are doing this alright. "Hello daddy. I have a question for you; I need you to tell me right now if I was your girlfriend or your daughter. Tell me right now because as far as I know, a girlfriend is someone you can meet and then decide to leave but your daughter is someone that has to be in your life no matter what. You brought a daughter into existence, so it means you must be responsible for her." I said very fast, very loudly in a tearfully cracking voice that was raw with emotion. "Go on my baby, shout it all out I am here listening. I am not going to hang up, okay, Tina? He spoke in a collected tone. So, I went on. "Where were you when all those boys told me that I have daddy issues when I couldn't let a relationship hold, where were you when I started doing DIY décor and furniture as you taught me, where were you when I started baking without that big oven you promised, where were you when I got pregnant and had to survive on Sorghum beer that Macum gave me because I had nothing to eat, where were you when another man was taking your daughter to school, answer me," and then I broke down. I don't think I ever cried so much in my life. I was choking on my cry and began to cough when I heard a cry that wasn't as loud and temperamental as mine; it was deep and sombre. Oh no, my father was crying; I had made my father cry. In a groggy and raspy voice, I said, "Daddy? I'm sorry, I didn't mean to make you cry. I didn't mean to shout at you those words just came out." "I am not crying because you were shouting Tina, I am crying because I don't have the answers to your questions. I am crying because you are right, and I had never looked at things that way. I stayed out of touch because I felt guilty for leaving you. My adult issues had nothing to do with you and I admit I was wrong." He said this sincerely with a deep sigh. "Tina I was wrong, and I am terribly sorry for all the pain my leaving you caused. I missed all those parts of your life, and I will make it up. I know I am a little too late but with what's left of me, I want to be a part of your life." He concluded and spoke. We both smiled; I'm sure I heard him smile into the phone. It felt as though a huge load had been removed from my shoulder. I felt lighter. This is what I needed; I didn't need to die; I needed to confront and address what was depressing me. I went back to Mai MaTshu and told her. We cried together tears of joy. I was happy again. I asked her other questions about my childhood that I had, and she answered them. We spent 4 days back and forth on the phone addressing everything. She brought colour to the grey areas in my life. All I needed was therapy and nothing is as therapeutic as love from family. We sometimes look far when our answers are right there in Infront of us. My father did become a part of my life. He asked if I was still hoping from boyfriend to boyfriend with my daddy issues and I told him I had met a man who loved me wholly. I introduced him to the man who had changed my life. I told him all about this man who met me and loved me totally, with all my brokenness. When I met him and my issues took over, he sat me down and said, Tina no, we are not breaking up because of a petty misunderstanding. You cannot up and leave every time you get into conflict, you tackle it head-on, and you do not run. If you do this every time you would date 20 men because they will all come with conflict. That is what life does." He fought for me. That's something no one has ever done in my life. He went on and spoke. "Allow me to love you, Tina. I want to love you until you love yourself." I melted. He didn't lie; he loved me with a deepness I could not fathom until I understood what love is. He moulded me into the woman I am today with his patience and unconditional love. I remember one of my aunties saying to him, "Thank you for loving Tina; I know she is difficult to love but you do it ever so effortlessly." He became the reason I wanted to become a better person. It is easy to love someone when they are a good person who is trying to be perfect but to love someone who is flawed, who is a mess, who is damaged, I think that's what really allows you to see how much love there really is. I knew I needed to do some sort of levelling up for me to deserve his amorousness. His love for me awakened my soul and nothing I have ever wanted compared to what was being given to me. I proudly introduced him to my father via video call. As they smiled at each other and chatted away, I felt my heart filling in the gaps that were empty. As he confirmed to my father that he loves me, he looked at me and looked back at the man in the video and smiled. That moment when the two men I have ever absolutely loved; had deliberately chosen to love me, their smiles at each other silenced my fears. And, just when I thought I couldn't love any more than I already did, I felt myself sinking deeper into love because finally, everything now made sense.

Lest we forget, we are still in the Hagar season of my life. My child's prayers sustained us when I hit rock bottom. When Ishmael prayed, God answered his prayer; "And God heard the voice of the boy, and the angel of God called to Hagar from heaven and said to her, "What troubles you, Hagar? Fear not, for God has heard the voice of the boy where he is." Genesis 21:17. That must have felt like a hug to Hagar. In the same token, my prayer was answered momentarily after my child had prayed for me. Looking back, I now know why her name was whispered to me all those years ago. Remember I called her Chikomborero, meaning blessing, when I was still pregnant? God knew she would be a blessing. He is the God who sees. He had seen my future and gave me a child even when I thought I wasn't ready to have a child. Yes, we could say at that point I wasn't ready, but we won't be looking at what purpose my child is serving now. At that time when I was suffering while pregnant when people didn't understand why I wouldn't just abort so that I would go back to my normal life, she was given to me for a time like this. I honestly don't know what my life would have been if I didn't have my daughter with me. She is my voice of reason, my best friend, the best thing I never knew I needed, and she is my everything in between.

Chapter - 11

The Noah Season of My Life

"He brings into existence whatever exists:"

Yahweh!

The one who finishes what He starts, that Same God who won't let His word return to Him before it finishes what it was sent out to do. The keeper of covenants, the one who has no record of ever failing, the all-sovereign One. Adonai. The God who is there. He is worthy to be praised.

God's Perfect Timing.

"Yes doctor, I have already had an ultrasound and taken medication, but I don't understand why I still am not getting my monthly period," I said with frustration in my voice. I continued and said "Ok, so did you send that referral to the Gynaecologist's clinic? Maybe they will be able to figure out what is going on with me. He said he did twice, but I hadn't received a call from that clinic. I thought to myself, okay, so since science has failed to see what is going on with me, maybe I will try visiting a naturopathic doctor. I called that office, and she told me to buy chaste berry or raspberry leaf tea. I did, but still my period didn't come. I knew for a fact that I wasn't pregnant, but any woman would be concerned if she didn't have her period for months without being on any hormonal medication or contraception that hinders menstruation. I was confused. The doctors had seen nothing wrong, the blood work showed that all my hormone levels were fine and according to them, I must have been menstruating properly. If you have noticed, I never mentioned that I prayed about it. It is something simple that should just normally happen every month. I then resorted to prayer last. Yes, I didn't think it was a matter that was prayer worthy but boy, was I wrong! I went on my knees and spoke to the Father. I didn't even know what to say in prayer because it seemed far-fetched and then as I fumbled with words, I just felt this inclination to study Hannah. I wondered what any of this had to do with Hannah, so I took out my bible and began to study. I read everything that had to do with Hannah and still nothing. My mind was still just blank. I gave it another go and again, nothing. I turned to YouTube, listened to sermons about Hannah and still there wasn't that one thing that I could point to. It was different. I was now so invested that I couldn't let it go, so I called people that know the word and asked them to teach me about Hannah and still, nothing. Then as I was about to give up on this search for something I didn't know, I had a moment of revelation. It was a tiny part of scripture that said, "Because the LORD had closed Hannah's womb..." 1 Samuel 1:6. I screamed in excitement because I had finally found my answer. I was going round and round when my answer was right in front of me; I don't know how many times I had read that tiny part and didn't think that was what I need to focus on. So, I was answered; the Lord had closed my womb. But why?

God knows His people. When I got that vision of those children, I showed a deep level of desperation and the Lord knew that if He didn't put a leash on me, I probably would have started to find ways to try and get pregnant just so that I could manifest the vision myself. I won't lie to you; I was embarrassed because God literally called me out on this one. So, Him shutting my womb meant that I was going to focus on having a healthy menstrual cycle first before I could think of trying to find ways to get pregnant. The Lord saved me from myself, and I didn't even realize it until this moment. So, with that knowledge, I went back on my knees, with my face looking deep into the ground because there was no way I was lifting my head up to even look in the Lord's direction. Not with the way I was embarrassed and laughing at myself. So, God knew that I, His child was so forward, I would have found ways to just manifest the vision by myself and God wasn't going to let me destroy His wonderful plan for my life.

When God tells you something, it doesn't mean it isn't already existing in the spiritual realm; it is just waiting for God's perfect time for it to be made to exist in this physical realm. We have to wait for God to do what He does for Him to get it to us. Some things aren't only about us but involve other people, and God has to align everything in every dimension before anything tangible can happen.

God tells us beforehand because He wants us to prepare for what's to come. Being shown a vision doesn't mean it will happen within your time frame. God works in ways we cannot see, He already said, "For my thoughts are not your thoughts, neither are your ways my ways," As the heavens are higher than the earth, so are my ways higher than your ways and my thoughts than your thoughts." Isaiah 55:8-9

Let's use an example. Your child loves Tesla. Each time you guys drive past a tesla, you say to your child, "I will buy you that car. Do you know that money we've been putting aside in that account we don't touch? yes, that money is going to go towards your tesla." Did I mention your child is 13 years old? Then after having that conversation, your child doesn't let that thought leave their head. They now start to try and access that money so that they can buy that car themselves. Wouldn't you just want to slap them? You are a parent; you know the reason why you aren't buying the car today. They cannot drive yet; they aren't even allowed to have a driver's license. Yes, you will buy the car when the time is right. You are protecting them because if they drive now and get into an accident, they may damage their driving record and never be able to drive again. There are endless possibilities as to what might happen with an unlicensed 13-year-old on the wheel. God is to us a loving parent as we are to our children. He knew that this cunning child of His called Tina would find a way to get to that savings He told me about and try to buy the car herself. He gave me a very practical and literal lesson on waiting on His time. I learnt something big, something called Obedience. I stopped worrying about the period that wasn't coming and began listening to what it is the Lord was trying to teach me during this season.

Noah is what Obedience looks like

Surrendering to God's authority and basing our actions and decisions on what the word that God said about our lives must be one of the most challenging things there is. As people, it is in our nature to know how things are going to unfold before we get there. We always want to be in control, and we need to learn to let go and let God. "Faith and trusting in God is not comfortable, and it never gets comfortable because we as human beings are used to controlling things and we want to know how everything is going to turn out before we start out and faith is not being able to see, but it's an inner knowing that God has you, but you have to step out." (CeCe Winans)

Who would start planning for a wedding, choosing a gown, engaging caterers, and paying for a venue and things like that before you even have a boyfriend? Growing up my mother always used to tell me about a girl who did, but would you do it? It is illogical right? But to whom? It depends on who told you to plan. If it is you just fantasizing then you are in for a disaster, but if God tells you to do it, and you know it is really God who said it, then no matter how illogical it sounds, just do it! Sadly, our human mind is not wired that way. Let's bring this biblical giant called Noah into perspective.

The Lord said to Noah, "Make for yourself an ark of gopher wood; make rooms in the ark and coat it with pitch inside and out. And this is how you are to build it: The ark is to be 300 cubits long, 50 cubits wide, and 30 cubits high. You are to make a roof for the ark, finish its walls a cubit from the top, place a door in the side of the ark, and build lower, middle, and upper decks... And you are to bring two of every living creature into the ark—male and female—to keep them alive with you. Two of every kind of bird and animal and the crawling creature will come to you to be kept alive. You are also to take for yourself every kind of food that is eaten and gather it as food for yourselves and for the animals." So, Noah did everything precisely as God had commanded him. Genesis 6:14

Okay, we will do this very slowly. God told Noah to build an ark and to bring every living creature into the ark, and Noah just said, Okay? Noah could have asked, "But Lord, explain to me how I am going to get a lion and the lioness and tell them to leave their cubs and they actually come with me willingly? oh wait, how do I get the shark from the ocean, with its female and then walk from the ocean dragging the shark all the way into ark?" perhaps he could have said, wait Lord, the cheeter, how will I keep up with its pace to catch it and then find its other? How am I even doing all this without being killed by one of your animals?" What God told Noah to do was illogical but because Noah knew the God he serves, he didn't ask Him all those questions. He knew the kind of authority that God has over all of His creation. He knew that he was dealing with the Almighty God. Noah only had to do as he was told, no questions asked. The bible even says he did it precisely. Wow! Could we ever be like Noah? Could the Lord tell us something now and we do precisely what He says? We spent the entire book talking about how He is the Same God, but can that Same God count on us to have obedience as His people in the biblical days? What has changed? He is the Same God isn't He, we see Him in our lives today doing all these wonderful things as He did back in the day. We have seen from my life just how He has remained consistent, but we haven't spoken about your life; remember all those times that He showed up for you? Remember how He answered your prayer by giving you that one thing you had forgotten about. If He answered your prayer back then? What makes you think He will not answer this one? Look back, you may be living in your answered prayer right now but you forgot that you prayed for this because right now there is something else you are praying for. Did you take some time to enjoy this answered prayer for just a little while and thank Him for it?

Do we obey Him? Do we do as we are told, no questions asked?

I was challenged. The Lord knew my weakness and revealed it to me but loved me, nonetheless. My intrusive thoughts towards His plan for me didn't change because I had faltered. He understood He had to show me how I might have gotten in the way of His bigger picture for me. When I had learnt my lesson and He had seen that my heart was where He wanted it to be, He took it a step further and asked me to obey Him as Noah did. The Holy Spirit showed me a nursery in a vivid vision. I was then told to make that nursery. I didn't ask any questions. I didn't ask Him when my period would return or why I would be having a nursery before I am even married. Everything that is needed for me to have a child rightfully is currently absent but like Noah, I know the God I serve. I do not dwell on it. I have a beautiful nursery with all the beautiful neutral colours. I have even bought a first bible for the nursery, and I continue to work on it because I don't need to see my period to know that soon, everything will be in place. I don't need to see my tomorrow I just need to know that the maker of tomorrow has me exactly where He needs me to be. I walk by faith and not by sight because my Bible tells me in Romans 10:17, "So then, faith comes by hearing and hearing by the word of God." The Word gives me faith to believe in what is promised because the Word was with God and the Word was God. (John 1:1)

God may show you a vision of where you will end up, but that may not include how you will get there. Often, when something is revealed to us, we look at our current circumstances and tend to want to make a way for ourselves.

Let Go and let God Ephesians 3:20

Conclusion

We all have our different paths and different purposes. My journey may not be similar to your journey but ultimately, God has a plan and a purpose for all of us. What we need to do is to find Him and we strive to know what our purpose is. Getting to fully understand what God wants you to do takes a lot of learning and unlearning. It takes pain as you pass through harrowing situations that are meant to shape you. I have learnt from experience that if I know which biblical character my current circumstances resemble, I have a bit of an idea of what I am in for. If you look and feel that maybe you are in the Azariah/Abednego season of your life, then you know that you are in for one raging fire. You prepare yourself to go into the fire because you know that another will be with you in it. You pray accordingly. So instead of praying and asking God to put out the fire, you pray and ask Him to be with you in it so that when you emerge, you are like a diamond that is forged by fire.

To become it, you must go through the fire. Life is hard, we live in a world that wants to swallow us whole and we have to try our best to not be consumed. If we do this life with the Lord ordering our footsteps, it will still hurt but we will have hope. We know that God will not let us suffer without a reward in the end. He will wipe your tears and will give you happiness that is in proportion to the misery that you went through. He will replace the bad years with good ones (Psalms 90:15)

Sometimes when we pray for something and we dwell on it, we are causing ourselves to be miserable. Pray about and then let God do the rest. Move on to another thing and remove your focus on what you have no control over. Let God be in control means you don't do part of the thing and then expect God to meet you halfway. The Lord doesn't need a personal assistant. Once you leave a situation in His hands, stop trying to meet Him halfway. Surrender it all and let Him show you why He is the King of kings and Lord of lords. What He has meant for you will always find its way to you without you needing to help Him to bring it forth.

In honour and loving memory of my grandmother Mrs. Hedwig Raradza.

May she rest in peace.

This picture summarizes our Relationship. She taught me a lot and I owe her so Much.

About Kharis Publishing:

Kharis Publishing, an imprint of Kharis Media LLC, is a leading Christian and inspirational book publisher based in Aurora, Chicago metropolitan area, Illinois. Kharis' dual mission is to give voice to under-represented writers (including women and first-time authors) and equip orphans in developing countries with literacy tools. That is why, for each book sold, the publisher channels some of the proceeds into providing books and computers for orphanages in developing countries so that these kids may learn to read, dream, and grow. For a limited time, Kharis Publishing is accepting unsolicited queries for nonfiction (Christian, self-help, memoirs, business, health and wellness) from qualified leaders, professionals, pastors, and ministers. Learn more at: https://kharispublishing.com/